Auto Repair Made Simple

Step-by-Step Maintenance and Expert Tips for Every Driver

AUTHOR: **The Books of Pamex**

TABLE OF CONTENTS

Chapter 1: Foundations of Car Maintenance and Systems — 7

VEHICLE COMPONENTS AND SYSTEMS: DIAGRAMS & ANALOGIES — 13

Chapter 2: Essential Tools and Workspace Safety — 19

Chapter 3: Routine Maintenance Planning & Scheduling — 23

VEHICLE INSPECTION SCHEDULES AND CHECKLISTS — 28

Chapter 4: Engine Oil, Care, and Wear Signs — 33

Chapter 5: Cooling System Components and Coolant Care — 38

Chapter 6: Battery Maintenance & Electrical Diagnostics — 42

Chapter 7: Brake Inspection, Maintenance & Replacement — 46

CHAPTER 8: 4 TIRE MAINTENANCE AND REPAIR PROJECTS — 49
- Checking Tire Pressure and TPMS Diagnostics — 49
- Measuring Tread Depth and Rotating Tires — 50
- Puncture Repair: Plug and Patch Method — 53
- Mounting, Balancing, and Valve Stem Replacement — 55

CHAPTER 4: TIRE MAINTENANCE AND REPAIR PROJECTS — 57
- Tire Inspection and Cleaning for Longevity — 57

Seasonal Tire Changeover and Proper Storage	59
Locating and Repairing Slow Leaks and Bead Seals	62
Safe Tire Removal and Full Replacement with a Spare	64

CHAPTER 9: 4 FLUID CHECKS AND REPLACEMENT PROJECTS — 66

Engine Oil Change and Filter Replacement	66
Coolant System Flush and Refill	69
Brake Fluid Inspection and Replacement	71
Automatic Transmission Fluid Check and Service	73

4 FLUID CHECKS AND REPLACEMENT PROJECTS — 76

Power Steering Fluid Inspection and Replacement	76
Rear Differential Fluid Change and Seal Inspection	78
Transfer Case Fluid Check and Replacement	81
Windshield Washer System Flush, Nozzle Cleaning, and Refill	83

CHAPTER 10: LIGHTING AND ELECTRICAL FIX PROJECTS — 85

Headlight Bulb Replacement and Beam Alignment	85
Taillight, Brake Light, and Turn Signal Socket Repair	88
Interior Dome and Courtesy Light Switch Replacement	90
Fuse Box Diagnosis and Corroded Connector Repair	92

4: LIGHTING AND ELECTRICAL REPAIR PROJECTS — 95

Daytime Running Light Troubleshooting and Module Replacement	95
LED Headlight Retrofit and Beam Pattern Adjustment	98
Alternator Output Test and Voltage Regulator Replacement for Charging Repairs	100
Chassis Ground and Wiring Harness Corrosion Repair for Lighting Circuits	103

CHAPTER 11: TROUBLESHOOTING COMMON ENGINE PROBLEMS — 105

No-start diagnosis and starter relay replacement	105
Cylinder misfire diagnosis with spark plug and ignition coil service	108
Engine overheating diagnosis with thermostat and water pump replacement	110
Rough idle troubleshooting with intake manifold and vacuum leak repair	113

4 TROUBLESHOOTING COMMON ENGINE PROBLEMS — 116

Cold and hard-start diagnosis — fuel pump, filter and pressure test — 116

Excessive exhaust smoke diagnosis — oil burning, coolant leak and injector check — 119

Engine knock and ping troubleshooting — knock sensor, timing and octane fixes — 121

Loss of power diagnosis — clogged catalytic converter, MAF and throttle body service — 123

CHAPTER 12: 4 PREVENTIVE MAINTENANCE PROJECTS — 126

Scheduled Maintenance Checklist and Service Interval Log — 126

Battery Inspection, Load Test and Terminal Cleaning — 128

Serpentine and Timing Belt Inspection with Tensioner Check and Replacement — 130

Engine Air Filter and Cabin Filter Replacement with Intake and Ventilation Cleaning — 133

4 PREVENTIVE MAINTENANCE PROJECTS — 135

Monthly Preventive Maintenance Walkaround and Digital Log — 135

Cooling System Hose, Clamp and Radiator Care with Pressure Test — 138

Brake System Preventive Service: Pad Measurement, Caliper Lubrication and Rotor Dressing — 140

Electrical System Preventive Check: Corrosion Control, Grounding and Connector Sealing — 143

CHAPTER 13: FOUR INTERIOR & EXTERIOR CARE PROJECTS — 145

Leather Seat Cleaning, Conditioning, and Small Tear Repair — 145

Fabric Upholstery Stain Removal and Odor Neutralization — 147

Interior Plastic and Vinyl Restoration with UV Protectant — 149

Exterior Paint Scratch Touch-Up, Clear Coat Blending, and Polishing — 151

4 INTERIOR AND EXTERIOR CARE — 154

Carpet and Floor Mat Deep Clean with Odor Neutralization — 154

Dashboard and Console Crack Repair with UV Protection — 156

Convertible Top Cleaning, Waterproofing and Zipper Service — 158

Exterior Trim and Chrome Polish with Pitting Repair — 160

Chapter 14: Troubleshooting, Resources, Next Steps — 164

© 2025 The Car Maintenance and Repair Bible

All Rights Reserved

This document is intended solely for informational purposes and relates to the book titled The Car Maintenance and Repair Bible.

Unauthorized reproduction, distribution, or transmission of this book, in whole or in part, is strictly prohibited.

All trademarks and brand names appearing in this book are the property of their respective owners.

The publisher disclaims all responsibility for any damages, losses, or injuries that may result from the use or misuse of the information contained herein.

The book is provided "as is" without any warranties, express or implied, including but not limited to implied warranties of merchantability, fitness for a particular purpose, and non-infringement.

No guarantee is made that the information is complete, accurate, up-to-date, or applicable to any specific vehicle, situation, or jurisdiction.

Users are advised to seek professional guidance and to verify information before applying it to real-world maintenance or repair scenarios.

Reliance on any content from this book is at the reader's own risk, and the publisher shall not be liable for any damages arising from such reliance.

Chapter 1: Foundations of Car Maintenance and Systems

Tip

If you're just starting out with DIY car maintenance, focus on simple, confidence-building tasks like checking and topping off fluids, replacing air and cabin filters, and swapping wiper blades. These jobs are quick, require minimal tools, and help you get familiar with your car's systems. As you gain experience, you'll save money and be better prepared to tackle more complex repairs down the road.

It can feel overwhelming at first to learn how a car works, but breaking it down into its main systems makes it easier to grasp. Think of the vehicle as a well-orchestrated system where every part has a role. At the center is the **engine**, like the heart of a living being; just as the heart pumps blood to energize the body, the engine burns a specific mix of fuel and air to create the power needed to move the vehicle. Depending on the model, this can produce anywhere from **100 to 500 horsepower**.

Fuel and air intake act like the lungs, drawing in the oxygen and fuel needed to form a combustible mixture—usually about **14.7:1** air to fuel for optimal combustion. That mixture is ignited in the engine's cylinders, producing small explosions that push pistons down and turn the crankshaft at speeds that can exceed **6,000 RPM** in performance engines. The engine converts the chemical energy of fuel into mechanical energy, which propels the vehicle forward; many modern cars reach **0 to 60 mph in under 6 seconds**.

After the engine produces power, the **transmission** handles how that power is used, much like gears on a bicycle. You shift gears to make pedaling easier or harder depending on terrain; the transmission changes gear ratios to keep the engine running efficiently at speeds typically between 20 and 80 mph. It transfers power to the wheels through the **drivetrain**, which can be front-wheel, rear-wheel, or all-wheel drive—each setup offering different handling and traction characteristics.

Controlling that power requires **steering**, **suspension**, and **brakes**. The steering lets you guide the vehicle, similar to handlebars on a bike, and most modern systems include power assist for easier maneuvering. The suspension soaks up bumps and keeps the tires in contact with the road, usually using coil springs and shock absorbers for stability. Brakes control speed and stop the vehicle, using disc or drum systems that create friction; stopping distances can range from about **100 to 300 feet** depending on speed and road conditions.

Electrical and electronic systems coordinate everything from starting the engine to powering lights and infotainment. The battery and alternator supply and replenish electrical power—batteries are typically **12 volts** while alternators generate roughly **13.5 to 14.5 volts**. These systems are vital for modern vehicles, which rely on electronics for engine management, navigation, and increasingly for driver-assistance technologies.

Fluids keep the vehicle running smoothly. Coolant prevents the engine from overheating by circulating through the engine and radiator at temperatures that can exceed **200°F**. Oil reduces friction between moving parts and prevents wear; changing it every **5,000 to 7,500 miles** is generally recommended. Other fluids, like brake fluid and power-steering fluid, help operate the braking and steering systems, with brake fluid usually replaced every **two years** to maintain performance.

The body and interior provide structure and comfort. The body protects internal components and passengers and is often made from high-strength steel or aluminum to balance safety and weight. The interior offers a functional, comfortable space for driving, featuring ergonomic layouts and advanced infotainment systems.

Open the hood and you'll find the engine's service points clustered for easy access. The **oil dipstick** (often a bright yellow or orange handle) shows level: pull, wipe, reinsert fully, then pull again—the oil should fall between the two marks. Add oil at the **filler cap**, usually stamped with an oil-can icon; use the grade specified in your owner's manual.

A translucent **coolant reservoir** with a temperature-warning cap indicates coolant level—only open it when the engine is cold and keep fluid between the min and max marks. The **brake-fluid reservoir**, marked with a brake symbol, is similarly transparent so you can monitor level; maintain it within the indicated range.

The **air-filter box** (black plastic secured by clips or screws) houses the intake filter; it should be clean and debris-free. Replace per the manufacturer's interval—often around 12,000–15,000 miles, sooner in dusty conditions. The *cabin air filter*, which cleans incoming cabin air, is usually behind the glove box or under the dash and is commonly changed every 15,000–30,000 miles.

The **battery** is a rectangular unit with + and − terminals; keep those terminals tight and free of corrosion (a baking-soda-and-water paste removes buildup). The **serpentine belt** drives accessories such as the alternator and A/C compressor—inspect it for cracks, glazing, or fraying. Radiator hoses and other coolant lines should be checked for soft spots, cracks, or leaks, and the radiator face kept clear of debris.

Locate the **fuse box** (near the battery or under the dash) to check fuses when an electrical item fails. The **windshield-washer reservoir** is usually clear with a blue or black cap and a windshield icon—top it off as needed. The **OBD-II diagnostic**

port is typically beneath the driver's side dash; a scan tool reads fault codes to help identify problems.

Refer to the sticker in the driver's door jamb for recommended tire size and pressures—proper inflation aids safety, handling, and fuel economy. Know your jack points (found in the owner's manual) and where the spare and tools are stored (trunk floor or side compartment).

Exercise caution around hot parts, note labels and symbols on components, and avoid touching surfaces that retain heat. Regularly inspect hoses, belts, and connections and replace any that show wear to prevent breakdowns.

Photograph and label your engine bay—creating a simple map of key components speeds routine checks and makes future maintenance easier.

Preventive maintenance keeps the car reliable and helps avoid costly repairs by addressing small issues before they escalate. It consists of regular, simple tasks intended to extend component life and sustain performance. Rather than fixing failures after they occur, this proactive approach—**for example, routine oil service**—reduces wear and the risk of overheating that can lead to expensive engine work.

Follow the service intervals in your owner's manual for items like oil and filter changes, brake checks, and scheduled inspections. Many vehicles provide dashboard reminders based on mileage or elapsed time. Adjust those intervals for *severe use*: frequent short trips, towing, or extreme temperatures often call for more frequent attention—sometimes reducing recommended intervals by roughly a quarter.

Keep consumables up to date and perform routine inspections. Change oil and its filter per the manufacturer (*synthetic oils may allow longer spans*). Monitor coolant and brake fluid and top or replace them as required. Service steering fluid on vehicles that use it and change transmission fluid at the recommended mileage to preserve shifting quality. Replace engine and cabin air filters on the manufacturer's schedule to protect engine components and cabin air quality. Check spark plugs when due to maintain engine efficiency and swap wiper blades at least annually for good visibility.

Tires need regular care: check tread depth, maintain the correct inflation listed on the door jamb sticker, and rotate them to encourage even wear—typically every several thousand miles. Inspect the battery for clean, tight terminals and consider periodic capacity testing. Small signs often indicate larger problems: unusual noises can signal worn brakes or belts, puddles under the car suggest leaks, odd odors may point to overheating or coolant issues, and dashboard warnings should be addressed promptly. Vibrations or hard starts also warrant inspection.

Make quick monthly checks of fluid levels and condition—look for discoloration or burnt smells—and verify electrical connections are secure. Measure tire pressure regularly; underinflation harms fuel economy and accelerates wear. These simple habits reduce breakdown risk and help your vehicle perform as intended.

Safety is essential when working on a vehicle. Allow hot components to cool before opening the hood—give it time to avoid burns—and avoid touching surfaces that retain heat. When handling electrical work, disconnect the **negative battery terminal** first to reduce the risk of shorts or sparks. Use properly rated **jack stands** on firm, level ground when lifting the car, and always support the vehicle at the manufacturer's recommended points. Wear **eye protection**, chemical-resistant gloves, and keep a well-ventilated workspace when running the engine to prevent carbon monoxide buildup.

Gather the right tools before you begin. A **tire-pressure gauge** (digital for best accuracy), a basic socket and wrench set in both metric and SAE, flathead and

Phillips screwdrivers, pliers, and a torque wrench are fundamentals. Include a funnel and drain pan for fluids, a work light (roughly 500 lumens or more), lint-free rags, and gloves. For electrical and diagnostic tasks, a **multimeter** and an **OBD-II scan tool** are indispensable.

Use diagnostic aids and organized records to stay on top of maintenance. Pay attention to dashboard warnings and scan fault codes when they appear. Keep a maintenance log—dates, parts, and observations—and follow a simple checklist for routine tasks (oil changes, tire rotations, brake checks) to avoid oversights.

If you're new to DIY maintenance, begin with straightforward jobs: check and top fluids, replace air and cabin filters, swap wiper blades, and inspect tires. Most of these take less than an hour, build confidence, and help you learn the car's systems. Record everything you do to simplify future troubleshooting and preserve vehicle value.

VEHICLE COMPONENTS AND SYSTEMS: DIAGRAMS & ANALOGIES

> **Tip**
> *For budget-conscious DIYers, start by learning to check and replace easy-to-access parts like air filters, spark plugs, and fuses. These simple tasks can prevent bigger issues, save you money, and build your confidence. Always consult your owner's manual for part locations and recommended intervals. Keeping a basic toolkit and gloves handy makes routine checks less intimidating and more efficient. Remember, small preventive steps go a long way toward avoiding costly repairs down the road.*

Imagine your engine as a clever pump that inhales air and fuel, ignites the mix, and then pushes the pistons to create motion. Think of it as a person breathing: taking in energy from the air to do work and then exhaling. Its main job is to transform the chemical energy in fuel—often measured in **BTUs** (British Thermal Units)—into mechanical energy that moves your car forward, usually expressed in **horsepower** or **torque**.

Now look at the parts and how they work together. Picture a labeled diagram where the pistons serve as the pump's arms, moving up and down in the cylinders, which are the chambers where combustion happens. These pistons connect to the crankshaft, similar to the main axle of a bicycle, converting straight motion into rotation that ultimately turns the wheels, often at several thousand **RPM** (revolutions per minute).

Air enters through the air filter, which works like the lungs' filter, keeping dirt out of the system. This air then flows through the throttle body, which acts like a faucet, controlling how much air enters. The more you press the accelerator, the wider the throttle opens, allowing more air in, measured in cubic feet per minute (**CFM**).

After the throttle body, the air moves into the intake manifold, a network of passages that evenly distributes air to each cylinder. Fuel is injected into the air stream by the fuel injectors, which deliver the right amount of fuel to form a combustible mix with a specific **air-fuel ratio**, usually about **14.7:1** for gasoline engines. The spark plugs ignite this mixture, causing a rapid expansion of gases that drives the pistons down with significant force.

The camshaft and crankshaft coordinate timing; the camshaft controls when the valves open and close, letting air and fuel in and exhaust gases out. A timing belt or chain keeps the camshaft and crankshaft aligned, usually within a few degrees, preventing pistons from striking valves, which could cause serious damage.

After combustion, exhaust gases leave the cylinders into the exhaust manifold, pass through the catalytic converter—which uses a chemical reaction to reduce harmful emissions like nitrogen oxides and hydrocarbons—and exit through the muffler, which reduces noise.

A beginner-friendly diagram could use *blue* for air, *red* for fuel, *gray* for exhaust, and arrows to show flow. Moving parts such as pistons and crankshafts might be highlighted in yellow, with callouts to common DIY spots:

- air filter box (easy to check and replace)
- MAF (Mass Air Flow) sensor (measures incoming air)
- throttle body (may need cleaning to prevent rough idling)
- spark plugs and coil packs (essential for ignition)

Knowing these components helps you diagnose simple issues. A rough idle can indicate an air leak in the intake or a dirty throttle body affecting airflow. If the car feels sluggish, a clogged air filter may be restricting airflow and reducing performance. Pinging noises can signal incorrect ignition timing or low-octane fuel, and a check engine light tied to a misfire could point to worn spark plugs or faulty coil packs, which would need further inspection.

Keeping your engine running smoothly means understanding how the **cooling**, **lubrication**, and **exhaust systems** interact. They collaborate to maintain performance and prevent damage. The following sections use simple diagrams and everyday examples.

Start with the **cooling system**. It's like your body sweating to cool off—the diagram shows coolant flow in blue. The **water pump**, acting like a heart, circulates fluid through the engine to carry away excess heat. The **thermostat** opens or closes to hold temperature in range; when the engine is hot it allows flow into the **radiator**. The radiator, with a fan, sheds heat to the surrounding air and the coolant returns to the reservoir to repeat the cycle.

Next, the **lubrication system** reduces friction and wear; its flow is shown in red. The **oil pump**, similar to a lotion dispenser, forces oil through passages to coat bearings, the camshaft, and other components, forming a protective film. After circulating, oil drains to the pan and passes through the **oil filter**—like *a coffee filter* removing debris—before being recirculated. Add icons for heat and friction to highlight where lubrication matters most.

The **exhaust system** routes combustion gases out of the engine, through emissions hardware that reduces pollutants, and finally through the **muffler** to quiet the sound. **Oxygen sensors** monitor the air–fuel mixture so the engine can adjust combustion for efficiency and lower emissions.

Common causes of overheating include low coolant, a stuck thermostat, or a failed radiator fan. If the oil-pressure warning lights up, low oil or an oil pump problem may be the issue—check the dipstick for level and contamination and look for leaks under the car. A burning smell or blue smoke can mean oil is entering the combustion chamber; a rotten-egg scent can indicate a failing catalytic component.

Simple owner checks:
- Inspect the coolant reservoir and hoses for cracks or leaks.

- Confirm radiator fans engage at operating temperature.
- Use the dipstick to monitor oil level and condition.

The transmission and drivetrain transfer the engine's power to the wheels. Between the engine and transmission you'll find either a **clutch** (manual) or a **torque converter** (automatic): the clutch disconnects the engine to permit gear changes, while the torque converter uses hydraulic coupling to allow automatic shifting under varying speed and load.

Inside the gearbox, different gear ratios match engine output to driving conditions so the vehicle moves efficiently. From the transmission, torque travels via the driveshaft or constant-velocity (CV) axles to the **differential**, which apportions power between wheels and allows them to turn at different speeds during cornering.

Suspension and steering systems keep the ride controlled and predictable. Springs and struts support the vehicle and absorb impacts; shock absorbers or struts dampen bounce. Control arms and tie rods link the wheels to the chassis for accurate steering input, and an anti-roll (sway) bar limits body roll in turns. **Power steering**—hydraulic or electric—reduces the effort required to turn the wheel, and correct wheel alignment prevents uneven tire wear and poor handling.

Braking starts at the pedal, which actuates the booster and master cylinder to pressurize brake fluid. That fluid moves to calipers (disc brakes) or wheel cylinders (drum brakes). Calipers squeeze pads against rotors to create stopping friction; drum systems use shoes pressing outward on a rotating drum. **ABS** rapidly modulates pressure to avoid wheel lockup and preserve steering control during hard stops.

Symptom clues:
- Vibration when braking often means warped rotors.
- Pulling to one side can be a sticking caliper, air in lines, or an alignment fault.
- Clunks over bumps usually point to worn bushings.

- Clicking on turns often signals a failing CV joint.
- Delayed or slipping shifts commonly relate to low transmission fluid or pressure issues.

Routine inspections—fluid checks, wear-item replacement, and prompt attention to the symptoms above—help prevent more serious failures and extend component life.

The vehicle's electrical system functions like a nervous network, supplying and controlling the power needed for operation. The **battery** sits at the core, storing energy to start the engine and run accessories when the engine isn't turning. Most cars use a 12-volt lead-acid battery; regular inspection and cleaning of terminals help ensure dependable starts. A simple wiring diagram shows the battery feeding circuits protected by fuses and switched by relays; **fuses** stop overloads, while **relays** let small control currents switch heavier loads.

Turning the key energizes the **starter motor** to crank the engine. Afterward, the **alternator**, driven by the engine, generates current to replenish the battery and support electrical systems while the vehicle runs. Weak lights or hard starting often trace to a discharged battery or poor **grounding** — the return path for current.

Modern vehicles rely on a network of sensors and control modules to monitor and adjust operation. Devices such as *O2 sensors*, the *mass-airflow sensor*, *MAP (manifold absolute pressure) sensors*, *coolant-temperature sensors*, and *wheel-speed sensors* feed information to the engine's control module (ECM/PCM). These modules communicate over a **CAN bus** so subsystems can coordinate and meet emissions and performance targets.

Comfort and convenience systems also depend on this electrical backbone. The **HVAC system** pulls cabin air through a filter; a blower forces it across the heater core or A/C evaporator before it's delivered through the vents. If the fan only works on the highest setting, suspect a faulty **blower-motor resistor**. Improper A/C or recirculation settings often cause window fogging — adjust controls to match outside conditions.

Other powered items include windshield wipers and washers, exterior and interior lighting, and infotainment gear. A dashboard **battery-or-charging warning** usually signals a problem in the charging circuit — frequently the alternator or its wiring.

Basic electrical checks you can do:
- Measure battery voltage with a multimeter (roughly 12.6 V with the engine off; about 13.7–14.7 V while running).
- Verify tight, corrosion-free terminals and grounds.
- Consult the fuse map to locate and test blown fuses and always replace fuses with the correct amperage to avoid fire risk.

Chapter 2: Essential Tools and Workspace Safety

If you plan to do DIY car repairs, the right tools and equipment make the work safer and smoother. Beginners should start with a solid set of essentials to handle a range of tasks. Below are the core hand tools and safety gear to begin with.

Start with a comprehensive metric and SAE socket set that includes **1/4-inch, 3/8-inch, and 1/2-inch drives** so you cover most jobs. Include both shallow and deep sockets for different bolt lengths to give you flexibility. Ratchets are necessary for using the sockets; a few extensions (3, 6, and 12 inches) plus a universal joint help reach bolts in tight spots. Combination wrenches, with an open and a box end, are essential for loosening and tightening nuts in cramped areas.

For screwdrivers, get a set with Phillips and flathead tips in various lengths—from stubby (about 3 inches) to long (up to 12 inches)—to suit different tasks. Pliers should include needle-nose for precision, slip-joint for general use, locking pliers for holding parts securely, and diagonal cutters for wire work. Keep hex (Allen) and Torx bits, typically *T10 to T50*, for interior and engine fasteners. An adjustable wrench covers odd sizes, while an 18-inch (or longer) breaker bar provides extra leverage on stubborn fasteners. A **torque wrench that reads 5 to 100 ft-lb** is crucial to tighten bolts to manufacturer specs, especially for wheel lug nuts.

Service aids speed up many jobs. An oil filter wrench removes filters cleanly, and a funnel plus a lidded drain pan make fluid changes neater. A fluid transfer pump helps refill or extract liquids from tight spots like a transmission. Hose clamp pliers remove and install clamps without damage. Trim clip removers and pry bars let you remove interior panels and trim without harming surfaces. A rubber mallet helps seat parts gently, while a magnetic pickup tool and a telescoping mirror retrieve dropped items and inspect hidden areas. Keep a panel fastener assortment for broken clips, and store thread locker and anti-seize for secure, serviceable fasteners. Penetrating oil loosens rusted bolts, and dielectric grease protects electrical connections from moisture. Shop towels and hand cleaner keep the work area tidy.

For measuring and diagnostics, a tire pressure gauge and tread depth gauge help maintain tires—most vehicles run around 30–35 PSI. A multimeter with continuity and DC voltage settings is key for electrical troubleshooting. A test light quickly checks for circuit power. An OBD-II scanner, even a basic unit, reads and clears trouble codes and shows live sensor data. An infrared thermometer diagnoses overheating by measuring surface temps, and feeler gauges measure gaps like spark plug gaps (typically 0.028–0.060 inches). A caliper or ruler and a straightedge assist with precise measurements and checking straightness.

To lift and support the vehicle safely, use a hydraulic floor jack rated above your vehicle's GVWR—2 tons is a common minimum for passenger cars. Pair it with properly rated jack stands (at least 3 tons) to hold the vehicle while you work. Wheel chocks prevent rolling, and plastic or rubber ramps provide quick undercarriage access. A kneeling pad or creeper makes working underneath the car more comfortable.

Safety gear is essential: safety glasses protect your eyes, nitrile and mechanic's gloves shield hands from chemicals and sharp edges, and hearing protection limits noise exposure from power tools. Use a dust mask or respirator when handling brake dust or solvents. Wear steel-toe or sturdy shoes to protect feet, and keep a Class B:C fire extinguisher for flammable-liquid fires. Maintain a first-aid kit stocked with bandages, antiseptic wipes, and basic supplies.

For lighting and power, a headlamp or trouble light gives hands-free illumination, and an LED shop light provides bright, even coverage. Use extension cords with

GFCI protection when running power tools. A battery maintainer or charger keeps the battery healthy, and jumper cables or a jump pack get a dead battery started.

Keep consumables on hand: a fuse assortment, spare bulbs, wire terminals, heat-shrink tubing, zip ties, electrical tape, Teflon/PTFE tape, RTV gasket maker, and replacement drain plug washers. Choose six-point sockets for better grip, invest early in a torque wrench and multimeter for accurate work, buy sets for better value, and store tools in labeled cases to avoid mix-ups.

Set up a safe, efficient workspace before you begin. Work on a level surface in a well-ventilated area—garage or driveway—leaving roughly three feet around the car for access. When using solvents or running the engine, increase airflow with open doors or a high-capacity fan; in hot weather, seek shade or use a portable fan. Protect the ground with spill mats or heavy cardboard.

Lighting and power should be reliable: bright LED overheads plus adjustable task lights for the engine bay and underside. Use surge-protected strips and cord reels, and prefer **GFCI-protected outlets**; route cords to eliminate trip hazards.

Keep tools and small parts orderly. A rolling chest with labeled drawers, a pegboard, or magnetic trays keeps frequently used items handy; use labeled bins for fasteners and dedicated shelves with secondary-containment trays for chemicals. Protect finishes with fender covers and keep service information—manuals or a tablet—nearby for torque specs and procedures.

Prioritize safety equipment: an appropriate fire extinguisher, a stocked first-aid kit, and an eyewash bottle. Before lifting, chock wheels and place stands on solid ground; follow the owner's manual for jacking points, never trust a jack alone, and perform a stability check before working underneath.

Handle fluids and hazardous materials correctly. Maintain **SDS files**, store fuels and solvents in approved, labeled containers, and use drip pans when transferring liquids. Keep used rags in a metal, lidded container and take waste oil, coolant, batteries, and other disposables to proper recycling facilities rather than dumping them.

Prepare and verify before starting a task:
- Stage tools, parts, and new fluids.
- Photograph disassembly steps and keep fasteners organized by step.
- Use a calibrated torque wrench for final tightening, inspect hoses and connections for leaks after reassembly, and take a brief road test to confirm systems.
- Clear any service reminders or diagnostic codes as needed.

For seasonal care, control the workspace climate—heater, fan, or dehumidifier as appropriate—and store batteries and electronics in weatherproof containers. Keep a charged jump pack available, especially in cold months when battery failures are more common.

Chapter 3: Routine Maintenance Planning & Scheduling

Tip

Start your maintenance journey with a simple service log. Whether you use a notebook or a free app, tracking each oil change, filter swap, and tire rotation builds your confidence and saves money. Set reminders for key intervals—like oil every 5,000 miles or air filters every 30,000. This habit not only helps you catch issues early but also boosts your car's resale value by showing a clear maintenance history.

To keep your car running smoothly and avoid breakdowns, set up a solid maintenance plan and begin with a baseline inspection. Start by creating a service log. Use paper or an app—whatever works best. Include the date of service, current mileage, and the specific tasks completed, such as oil changes, tire rotations, and filter replacements. Set reminders based on mileage and time intervals to follow the factory service schedules in your owner's manual. For example, change the oil about every **5,000 miles** or the air filter every **30,000 miles**.

Next, inspect your vehicle's fluids to establish a baseline. Begin with the engine oil—check level, color, and smell. Fresh oil is usually amber and neutral; dark or burnt-smelling oil indicates a change is due. Use the dipstick: the level should sit between the minimum and maximum marks. Then inspect the coolant in the reservoir; it should be bright and clear with no debris. A sweet smell is normal, but a burnt odor is a warning. Brake fluid should be clear or slightly yellow; dark fluid needs replacement. If your car has power steering, verify that fluid is clear and clean. For serviceable transmission fluid, expect a pinkish-red color and a slightly sweet scent; cloudy or burnt fluid requires changing. Also check windshield washer and differential fluids for proper levels and any cloudiness or sediment.

After fluids, assess wear items that affect performance and safety.

- Start with the tires—use a gauge to measure tread depth and confirm at least **2/32 inch**. Worn tires reduce traction and increase stopping distance.
- Measure tire pressures, including the spare, with a reliable gauge; proper inflation boosts fuel efficiency and improves handling and safety.
- Inspect wiper blades for cracks or wear that could reduce visibility.
- Test all exterior bulbs and replace dim or burned-out lights.
- Check the engine air filter and cabin filter, replacing them if dirty or clogged to protect engine performance and cabin air quality.
- Examine accessory belts for fraying or cracks.
- Test the battery's age, voltage, and charge with a multimeter to ensure reliable starts.
- Peek through the wheel spokes to assess brake pads and rotors for thickness and scoring or uneven wear.

During these inspections, watch for leaks or strange noises. Look under the car for fresh drips, which could signal leaks in the engine, transmission, or other systems—finding them early prevents larger repairs later. Inspect hoses for swelling or cracks that can lead to fluid loss and system failures, particularly in cooling and braking systems. Listen for odd sounds, such as squealing belts or grinding during turns, which can indicate worn parts. Document findings with photos and list any parts you need to order for replacement.

Establish a practical maintenance rhythm tied to miles and months.

Each month, do a quick check: confirm tire pressures at the recommended PSI, top off washer fluid, and scan under the hood for adequate engine oil, coolant, and brake fluid. Verify all exterior lights and glance at wiper condition. These brief checks take about 15-20 minutes and catch minor issues before they grow.

Every three to six months (roughly 3,000-6,000 miles), perform a deeper service. Replace oil and its filter per the owner's guidance and adapt frequency to your driving (frequent short trips or harsh climates mean shorter intervals). Rotate tires for even wear following the vehicle maker's pattern, and, with wheels removed, inspect pads, rotors, and tread depth. Clean battery terminals to prevent corrosion and swap cabin and engine air filters if dirty.

Annually, or near 12,000–15,000 miles, carry out a full review. Check brake fluid moisture and age, align the wheels if wear is uneven, and inspect suspension links, tie rods, bushings, shocks, and struts for play or leaks. Look over the exhaust for perforation or leaks and replace wipers to ensure clear sight lines.

Every two to three years (or by the schedule in your manual), change coolant to guard against overheating and corrosion. Service the **PCV valve** if equipped, refresh transmission fluid and filter as recommended, and replace worn accessory belts. Don't forget external fuel filters where applicable, and follow manufacturer intervals for differential and transfer case fluids.

Prioritize safety items—**brakes**, **steering**, **tires**, and any detected leaks—and address them immediately. Shorten service intervals when operating in severe conditions (towing, dusty environments, extreme temperatures, or many short trips).

Perform routine walkaround and under-hood checks to catch small problems before they grow. Begin with the tires.

Measure cold pressure (before driving or several hours after parking) with a quality gauge and set PSI to the values on the driver's door placard. When swapping positions, follow the rotation scheme for your drive type to even out wear, and inspect tread across the face with a depth gauge—replace tires that approach the legal minimum. Look for irregular wear patterns (**cupping**, **feathering**) that suggest alignment or suspension attention. After reinstalling wheels, tighten lug nuts to the vehicle's specified torque and verify again after a short run.

Check engine oil on level ground after the vehicle has sat so oil drains back into the pan. The dipstick should show a level within the marks and oil that is free of heavy discoloration or grit; top with the grade your manual calls for. Inspect the coolant level in the overflow tank while cold; keep it between the low and high marks and never remove a hot cap. Use the correct premix when adding. Verify brake fluid condition and use the **DOT** rating indicated on the reservoir cap.

Move on to filters and breathing components. Swap a visibly dirty engine air filter and clear the airbox of debris; replace a clogged or odorous cabin filter to restore HVAC flow. Ensure each element is properly seated to avoid unmetered intake.

Test the battery with a voltmeter—resting voltage near **12.6 V** is healthy; charging voltage with the engine running should be in the mid 13s to mid 14s. Clean corroded clamps, protect connections with dielectric grease, and confirm the battery is firmly clamped.

Inspect belts and hoses for cracking, glazing, soft spots, bulges, or fraying; check the tensioner for smooth operation and replace any compromised parts. Peek at brake pad material through the caliper opening—thin pads or squeal indicators mean it's time to service the system—and note any brake pedal pulsation or pull for professional evaluation.

Finally, scan the underside for fluid seepage at seals and pans, torn CV boots or grease loss, and loose or corroded exhaust hangers and heat shields. Tighten or secure fasteners as needed so components remain properly supported.

When a service is complete, confirm the job before driving off. Warm the engine briefly—about five minutes of idle—and scan the work area (oil filter, drain plug, any moved hoses or connectors) with a bright flashlight for seepage or loose fittings. If everything looks dry, top and set fluid levels to the maker's recommended ranges: **engine oil**, **coolant**, **brake fluid**, **transmission fluid**, and any others you handled.

Clear or reset dash service reminders per the owner's instructions so future intervals remain tracked. Then take a short local test drive long enough for the engine to reach normal temperature; pay attention to handling, smells, vibrations, and noises that might signal an assembly issue.

After the drive, recheck the same spots for new leaks and verify fluid levels again. Record the service in your log: date, mileage, parts and fluids used (*brand, spec, amount*), torque values applied, and any observations about wear or potential problems. Keep receipts with the entry and note the next service due date.

If you scanned for codes, save freeze-frame data and code history before clearing resolved DTCs. Continue to monitor live parameters (engine temp, fuel trims, charging voltage) for trends that could reveal emerging faults.

Use observed wear to refine intervals—for example, rotate more often if front tires wear prematurely, or shorten oil-change frequency for mostly city driving. Finally, keep a basic roadside kit in the car:
- spare bulbs and fuses
- correct-viscosity oil and premixed coolant
- tire plug kit and portable inflator
- gloves and shop towels

VEHICLE INSPECTION SCHEDULES AND CHECKLISTS

A solid vehicle inspection schedule and thorough checks are essential for keeping your car in good condition and staying safe on the road. Follow a clear workflow and use a practical checklist to inspect your vehicle systematically, catch problems early, and keep everything running smoothly. Here's a friendly guide to help you build an effective inspection routine:

Begin with an exterior walkaround so you don't miss anything. Use a calibrated tire gauge to verify inflation and a tread depth gauge to measure tread; the minimum legal requirement in most areas is **1.6 mm**. Watch for uneven wear—cupping or feathering can indicate alignment or suspension problems. Inspect all exterior lights, including headlights, taillights, and turn signals, to confirm they work and are aimed correctly. Examine wiper blades for cracks or wear that could reduce visibility in rain, and replace them if they're over six months old.

Open the hood and inspect fluid levels: engine oil, coolant, brake fluid, and power steering fluid. Use a dipstick for the oil and ensure the level sits between the minimum and maximum marks. For coolant, use a refractometer or test strips to verify concentration and condition, matching manufacturer specifications. Inspect belts for fraying or cracking and clean any corrosion from battery terminals. Use a multimeter to test battery voltage; around **12.6 volts** with the engine off and **13.5-14.5 volts** when running indicates proper charging.

Move to the cabin and turn on the HVAC to confirm heating and cooling work, and smell for unusual odors that could point to mold or debris. Scan the dashboard for warning lights and address them with an OBD-II scanner for diagnostic trouble codes. Verify all seatbelts operate correctly and inspect interior lights and controls for wear or malfunction.

After the cabin checks, examine the undercarriage for leaks around the engine, transmission, and differential. Use a clean paper towel to help identify the source of any fluid. Inspect CV boots for tears or grease leaks that can lead to costly repairs. Check the exhaust for rust or damage that may cause leaks or increased emissions, and make sure all hangers are secure.

After the static checks, perform a road test. Note how the vehicle handles and listen for unusual noises, such as squealing brakes or grinding gears. Test the brakes for responsiveness—they should engage smoothly without pulling to one side—and confirm steering feels tight and precise. Recheck for new leaks or issues after the drive, especially around brake lines and suspension components.

Create a reusable checklist you can keep on paper or in an app. Include yes/no fields, measurement boxes for specific readings, and slots for photos to document findings. Set action thresholds, for example replacing tires with tread less than **3 mm** or changing brake fluid if moisture exceeds **3%**.

Allocate time blocks for different inspection levels:
- Quick check (10–15 minutes) monthly: tire pressures, fluid levels, and lights.
- Intermediate inspection (45–60 minutes) quarterly: brakes, belts, and battery.
- Comprehensive inspection (90–120 minutes) annually: full undercarriage inspection and road test.

Gather parts and tools beforehand to minimize downtime. Pre-stage essentials like a torque wrench, tread depth gauge, OBD-II scanner, multimeter, and brake fluid tester, and have personal protective equipment such as gloves and safety glasses ready.

Record the date, mileage, ambient temperature, and driving conditions to provide context for your findings. Attach labeled photos to visually document any issues and keep documentation clear and organized for future reference.

Set reminders for inspections based on time and mileage, with alerts at **80%** of the interval to give a buffer. Include seasonal tasks, like testing the battery before winter and checking the A/C system before summer, to prepare for changing conditions.

Use quality gates to ensure thoroughness by torquing all critical fasteners to manufacturer specifications after servicing and marking them with paint to indicate they've been checked. Do a final visual sweep before closing the hood to catch any missed items and confirm components are secure.

Establish escalation rules for safety-critical issues. If you find problems that could compromise safety—brake performance issues, steering play, or active fluid leaks—stop driving immediately until the issue is repaired or inspected by a professional.

Begin outside with a focus on the tires and exterior. Check cold tire pressure with a reliable gauge and compare to the placard on the door jamb. Measure tread depth across each tire and watch for uneven patterns—cupping, feathering, or shoulder wear—that point to alignment or suspension faults. Inspect sidewalls for cuts or bulges, confirm valve caps are present, and look over wheels for cracks or damage at the bead.

Verify all exterior lighting and signaling; walk around while a helper exercises the brakes and turn signals to confirm operation. Inspect wiper blades for cracking or separation and aim the washer nozzles so spray covers the windshield.

Open the hood on level ground and assess fluids. Use the dipstick for engine oil—confirm level and an absence of scorched odor; top with the grade recommended in the owner's manual if needed. Check coolant level and color in the reservoir while cold and test concentration to ensure proper freeze/boil protection; never open the cooling system when hot. Inspect brake fluid for level and clarity and test for moisture contamination; service if readings are high. Verify and, if accessible, check power-steering, transmission, and differential fluids for correct level and appearance. Refill the washer reservoir as required.

Examine belts and hoses for signs of age or damage—cracks, glazing, softness, or bulging—and ensure tensioners move smoothly. Note the age of rubber components, as they typically wear over a few years.

Evaluate the battery and charging system: confirm resting voltage and that the alternator raises voltage when running, clean any terminal corrosion, secure the battery, and check its service age. If starting is weak, perform a load or starter test.

Remove and hold the air and cabin filters up to a light to judge cleanliness; replace filters that block light or smell musty. Clean the airbox and confirm filters seat properly. Test HVAC airflow and mode selection across settings.

With wheels installed, inspect brakes and suspension. View pad remaining through caliper openings and listen for wear indicators; feel for rotor lips and check for fluid level changes that could signal pad wear or a leak. Do a bounce test at each corner to assess shocks and struts, and inspect tie-rod and ball-joint boots for tears or leaks. Note any clunks or looseness that appear during a short drive.

Safely raise the vehicle on stands or ramps, chock wheels, and scan the undercarriage. Look for fresh fluid leaks at pans and seals, torn CV boots, exhaust corrosion or loose hangers, and compromised fuel or brake lines—especially in areas exposed to road salt. Confirm splash shields and fasteners are secure.

In the cabin, cycle the key to ON to observe that warning lights illuminate and then extinguish after startup. Scan for stored or pending OBD-II codes and review freeze-frame data. Test HVAC temperatures, blower speeds, A/C engagement, and operation of horn, windows, mirrors, and locks.

Perform a road test to evaluate dynamic behavior. Listen for unusual noises on startup and while accelerating, check steering for responsiveness and lack of excessive play, and brake from a range of speeds to detect pulsation, pull, or noise. Monitor transmission shift quality and watch for vibrations at specific speeds that indicate balance or alignment issues. Use on-board instruments or a scanner to observe engine temperature and charging system behavior.

After driving, recheck for new drips and any fuel, coolant, or burning odors. Verify fluid levels again and torque any wheels that were removed. Reset service reminders per the manual and record findings, recommended actions, and due dates in the maintenance log.

Chapter 4: Engine Oil, Care, and Wear Signs

> **Tip**
> *Before starting your oil change, gather all your tools and supplies in advance—this saves time and prevents mid-job frustration. Double-check that you have the correct oil type, filter, crush washer or O-ring, and the right wrenches. Laying everything out beforehand helps you avoid costly mistakes and ensures a smooth, efficient process.*

A solid grasp of engine care is key to getting the best performance from your vehicle and helping it last. One of the most important aspects of maintenance is choosing the right oil and filter. Start by checking your owner's manual or the specification plate under the hood. Those sources tell you the correct oil viscosity, industry approvals, and OEM specs for your vehicle.

Viscosity matters when selecting oil. You'll often see ratings like 0W-20 or 5W-30; these numbers describe thickness and flow at different temperatures. The first number (the **"W" stands for winter**) shows cold-temperature viscosity, important for chilly starts. A lower value means easier flow in the cold, useful for short trips or cold climates. The second number shows high-temperature behavior, crucial for protecting the motor under heavy loads such as towing. Always follow the manufacturer's recommended viscosity range to keep the motor running smoothly and prolong its life.

Also check oil approvals and specifications. Look for standards like **API SP**, **ILSAC GF-6**, or **ACEA** ratings, which confirm the oil meets industry performance criteria. Some makers have their own specs—*VW 504.00*, *MB 229.5*, or *Dexos*, for example—designed for specific engines. Choose oil that meets these standards to keep your vehicle's warranty intact and ensure efficient operation.

The motor's design and the suggested oil-change interval also affect your choice. Modern motors, particularly turbocharged or direct-injection ones, usually benefit from synthetic oils. Synthetics provide better protection and can lengthen intervals between changes; they handle extreme temperatures well, suited for cold starts and high-heat running. Conventional or blended oils may be acceptable for older, non-turbo engines if you plan on more frequent changes. Make sure any oil you use is compatible with your motor.

For high-mileage motors that burn oil or leak, use high-mileage formulations. They include seal conditioners to reduce leaks and oil consumption; confirm compatibility with your vehicle.

Filter quality matters. The unit must match the thread size and diameter for your motor. Check the bypass PSI rating—the pressure that causes the filter to redirect oil if it clogs. For top-mounted filters, choose one with an **anti-drainback valve** to prevent oil from draining out when the vehicle is off and ensure fast oil pressure on startup. Avoid generic or no-name filters; they can collapse and damage the motor.

Before changing oil, have crush washers or O-rings ready; they're usually replaced to ensure a proper seal. Check torque specs for the drain plug and canister cap to avoid over-tightening and potential leaks or damage.

If you want to extend change intervals or better understand your motor's condition, use oil analysis kits. They provide insights into oil condition and wear patterns, helping you decide on maintenance and change schedules.

Gather all tools and supplies before you begin: the correct socket or wrench for the drain plug (common sizes are **10mm** or **13mm**), a **torque wrench** set to your vehicle's spec, and a **filter wrench** suited to your filter style (cup, strap, or can). Use a drain pan that exceeds the engine's capacity (often 4–8 quarts), a wide-mouth funnel to reduce spills, rags, and nitrile gloves. If you'll raise the car, use a hydraulic jack plus jack stands or ramps rated for the vehicle and chock the wheels. Have a new filter, replacement seal (*crush washer* or *O-ring*), and a degreaser or brake cleaner on hand. Confirm oil type, capacity, and recommended filter numbers from the service manual.

Warm the engine briefly (a few minutes) so the oil flows more readily, then shut it off and park on level ground. Remove the oil fill cap and dipstick to vent the crankcase, and secure the vehicle with wheel chocks; if lifted, support it at the factory points specified in the manual.

Place the drain pan under the oil pan and loosen the drain plug with the proper tool, taking care to avoid hot splashes. Allow the oil to drain completely; this can take several minutes. While it drains, inspect the oil for abnormal signs—metallic particles, a milky appearance, fuel odor, or heavy sludge—and note the volume removed to compare with the expected capacity.

When draining finishes, replace the drain plug seal and start the plug by hand before torquing it to the manufacturer's value (avoid overtightening to prevent damaged threads or pan). Remove a spin-on filter with a wrench, catching residual oil, and check the mounting surface for a leftover gasket. If the filter mounts upright, prefill it to reduce dry starts; lightly oil the new gasket, thread the filter by hand, and snug per the specified turn or torque.

For cartridge-style filters, install fresh O-rings in their grooves on the cap and torque the cap to the recommended setting.

Pour in new oil using the manual's capacity as a guide but initially leave about 0.2–0.3 L spare to prevent overfill. Replace the fill cap, start the engine briefly—the oil pressure indicator should extinguish quickly—and inspect around the drain plug and filter for leaks. After shutting the engine off, wait a couple of minutes for oil to settle, then check the dipstick and top to the full mark if needed. Reset the maintenance reminder following the vehicle's procedure or with a scan tool.

Log the service date, mileage, oil brand and grade, and filter part in your maintenance records and keep receipts. Store used oil in sealed containers and take both oil and drained filters to an appropriate recycling center—do not dispose of them in household trash or drains.

Early signs of wear let you intervene before repairs get expensive. Start with oil usage: if the vehicle consumes more than about **1 L every 1,500–2,000 km**, investigate worn piston rings or leaking valve seals. Observe the exhaust: bluish smoke on acceleration commonly signals valve-seal leakage, while blue smoke under heavy load may mean worn rings or turbo issues and often accompanies power loss and higher emissions.

Listen for abnormal sounds. A rattle at cold start can point to a failing **timing chain or tensioner** and the risk of timing misalignment. A persistent ticking usually originates in the lifters or valvetrain, suggesting lubrication problems or wear. A deep, RPM-dependent knock is frequently **rod-bearing** related. Pinging or knock under load indicates pre-ignition — *low-octane fuel* or carbon buildup are common causes and can quickly damage the engine if ignored.

Inspect the tailpipe and intake for smoke and unusual smells. Oil-burning shows as blue smoke and reduces efficiency; persistent white vapor with a sweet odor once the engine is warm often indicates coolant entering the combustion chambers (think head gasket trouble), and heavy black smoke points to an overly rich mixture and wasted fuel.

Look under the filler cap and on the dipstick: light brown varnish is normal, but thick, tacky deposits point to overdue changes or overheating and risk oil starvation. A creamy, paint-like film signals coolant contamination and requires immediate attention.

Pay attention to pressure indications. Repeated low oil pressure readings or a warning lamp that flashes at idle after a warm run are serious — possible **oil-pump failure** or advanced internal wear — and should be addressed promptly to avoid seizure.

Check plugs during service for combustion clues: oily plugs mean oil is entering the cylinders and causing misfires; sooty black tips indicate richness; hard, ashy buildup can result from oil additives or coolant ingestion and presages more trouble.

Also watch for coolant/oil crossover: rising coolant level with an oily sheen, oil that drops while appearing creamy, or continuous bubbling in the overflow are classic signs of a breached head gasket or similar failure and warrant immediate diagnosis.

Use diagnostic tests to confirm suspicions. Compression and leak-down checks evaluate sealing; a borescope lets you view cylinder walls for scoring; and periodic used-oil testing reveals metal wear, fuel dilution, coolant traces, and viscosity shifts — compare results to prior tests to detect worsening trends.

Chapter 5: Cooling System Components and Coolant Care

A good grasp of your vehicle's cooling system helps keep it running smoothly and extends its life. The system is a network of parts that work together to keep the engine between about **195°F and 220°F (90°C to 104°C)**. Below are the main components and how to check coolant levels and condition.

The **radiator** is the central component of the cooling system and sits at the front of the vehicle to get airflow while driving. The **radiator cap (pressure cap)** maintains system pressure—typically around **15 psi**—which raises the fluid's boiling point to roughly **265°F (129°C)** and helps prevent overheating. The **overflow or expansion reservoir** catches excess fluid as it expands when hot and returns it as the system cools, keeping levels stable.

The **water pump** circulates the coolant throughout the system, moving roughly 20–30 gallons per minute depending on engine speed; it's usually driven by a belt. The **thermostat** opens at about **195°F (90°C)** to regulate flow and keep the engine at its optimal temperature. The **heater core** transfers heat from the fluid to the cabin air, providing warmth and generally running at similar temperatures to the engine.

Cooling fans, either mechanical or electric, draw air through the radiator when the vehicle is stopped or moving slowly. They activate around **220°F (104°C)** to boost heat dissipation. **Hoses**—the upper and lower radiator hoses, heater hoses, and bypass hoses—connect the components; clamps hold them in place to prevent leaks under pressure.

Temperature sensors monitor the engine and send data to the engine control unit (ECU), which adjusts cooling system operation to avoid overheating. **Bleed**

points let trapped air escape, ensuring steady flow and preventing pockets that can disrupt circulation.

Know the different types of coolant and their properties. Most are based on ethylene glycol or propylene glycol and use chemistries like **Organic Acid Technology (OAT)**, **Hybrid Organic Acid Technology (HOAT)**, or **Inorganic Acid Technology (IAT)**. Use the type specified by the vehicle manufacturer—mixing types can cause sludge and corrosion that shorten component life.

Safety matters when working on the system. **Never open it while hot**; pressurized fluid can cause severe burns. Remember coolant is toxic—avoid skin contact and keep it away from pets.

Check coolant with a cold engine. The reservoir level should sit between the **MIN** and **MAX** marks. Inspect color and clarity: it should be bright green, orange, or pink depending on the type. Brown, rusty, or cloudy fluid indicates contamination; an oily sheen can point to a head gasket or oil cooler problem that needs further investigation.

Examine the radiator cap for a good gasket and firm spring; replace it if cracked or weak, since a bad cap can cause pressure loss and overheating. Squeeze hoses and feel for firmness; they should not be mushy or cracked. Look for swelling, abrasion, or leaks at hose ends. Dried crust or colored deposits around fittings, the water pump weep hole, radiator tanks, or heater core areas (*damp carpet or a sweet smell*) can indicate leaks that require attention.

Watch the vehicle's temperature behavior. The engine should reach normal operating temperature within 10–15 minutes, and the gauge should remain in the mid-range. Verify the cooling fans engage at idle after warming up to maintain proper operating conditions.

For a deeper check, perform a **pressure test** to find hidden leaks and use a **refractometer** to confirm freeze and boil protection per the manufacturer's specs (for example, a **−34°F (−37°C)** freeze point and about **265°F (129°C)** boil point). Test strips can assess pH and inhibitor levels to gauge fluid effectiveness.

Follow the manufacturer's service schedule; most recommend a coolant flush every **30,000-50,000 miles** or every **2-5 years** depending on coolant type. Flush the system when the fluid is degraded or contaminated, after major cooling system repairs, or when changing coolant types to ensure compatibility.

Collect all necessary items before starting: the correct coolant (OEM concentrate or premix), distilled water if mixing, a new thermostat and gasket, and a replacement pressure cap if due. Also have hose clamps, a catch pan (≈5 qt capacity), gloves, eye protection, absorbent material or a spill kit, a funnel or spill-free/burping funnel, shop towels, a torque wrench, and the vehicle's service manual for capacities, bleed locations, and torque values. Begin with a cold engine.

Park on level ground (or slightly nose-up per the manual) and set the heater to the hottest setting so the heater circuit is open. Remove any splash shields that impede access, then drain the system via the radiator drain cock or by disconnecting the lower radiator hose into your catch pan. Vent the system by opening the reservoir cap (and radiator cap only when cold). If fitted, remove engine block drain plugs for a more complete drain; collect used fluid in sealed containers for proper recycling.

If using a chemical flush, reseal drains, add distilled water and the approved flush product at the recommended dilution, run the engine to operating temperature with the heater on, let it cool, then drain. Rinse with distilled water, repeating run/cool/drain cycles until the rinse water is clear.

When reinstalling, close drains and replace crush washers or seals as required. Torque block plugs and other fasteners to the manual's specifications. Reconnect hoses and clamps, seating them correctly and tightening to prevent leaks. Prepare the coolant mixture to the specified concentration (commonly 50/50 unless directed otherwise) and, if desired, confirm freeze/boil protection with a refractometer.

Refill slowly through the radiator neck or a spill-free funnel and bring the reservoir to the MAX mark. Purge air by opening bleed screws and running the engine at moderate rpm with the heater on high until the thermostat opens and warm air flows steadily. Top off as bubbles subside; when bubbling stops, close the bleeds and maintain the filler level to avoid introducing more air. Confirm fans operate and the temperature stays within normal range.

Secure the caps, clean any spilled fluid with water and degreaser, and inspect for leaks around hoses, the radiator, pump, and thermostat housing. Drive for 10–15 minutes, let the car cool, then recheck and top off levels if necessary. Log the service date, mileage, coolant type/brand and concentration, and parts replaced. Deliver used coolant to an approved recycling center in clearly labeled, sealed containers kept out of reach of people and animals.

Chapter 6: Battery Maintenance & Electrical Diagnostics

Any DIY car enthusiast should know the basics of car batteries. They power the engine start and all electrical components—lights, infotainment, and sensors. Here's an overview of common types, key specifications, and safe, effective maintenance.

Start by identifying the type your vehicle uses. Common options are **flooded lead-acid** units with serviceable caps for topping electrolyte; **maintenance-free sealed** types that need no periodic checks; **Absorbent Glass Mat (AGM)** cells, which are durable and tolerate deep discharges for high electrical loads; and **Enhanced Flooded Batteries (EFB)** found on start-stop cars for improved cycling and durability over standard flooded units.

Labels show key specs: **Cold Cranking Amps (CCA)** indicate starting ability in cold weather; **Cranking Amps (CA)** reflect performance at about 80°F (27°C). **Ampere-hours (Ah)** measure capacity—how much current the battery can supply over time. Reserve capacity gives minutes of power if the alternator fails. Check the date code, since performance often drops after three to five years.

Always wear protective eyewear and gloves to guard against acid splashes and sparks. Keep flames away and never smoke near the battery—hydrogen gas from charging is highly flammable. When disconnecting, remove the negative terminal first to reduce short-circuit risk. Use an *OBD memory saver* if you need to preserve electronic settings during replacement. Neutralize acid spills with a baking soda solution. Batteries typically weigh 30–50 pounds; use a proper handle or tray when lifting.

Visually inspect the case for bulging, cracks, or leaks that signal internal damage. Check for corrosion or white/blue-green buildup on posts and hold-downs, which can impair conductivity. Ensure the unit is securely mounted and the tray intact to prevent movement. Examine cables for fraying, stiffness, or hidden green corrosion under the insulation. For AGM and EFB types, route venting correctly to avoid gas buildup and pressure issues.

To clean and protect terminals, first remove the cables—negative before positive—to lower shorting risk. Use a wire brush to remove corrosion from posts and clamps. Rinse with a baking soda and water solution to neutralize acid, then dry thoroughly. Apply a thin coat of dielectric grease or a dedicated protectant to slow future corrosion. Reattach clamps snugly, not overly tight, and fit protective boots if available. Secure the hold-down per manufacturer specifications.

If you have a serviceable flooded lead-acid unit, check the electrolyte with the engine off: remove caps carefully and make sure the plates are covered. Top with distilled water to the fill line if needed—do not overfill—and reseal the caps tightly.

Charge using a **smart charger** set for the specific type (flooded, AGM, or EFB). A slow charge of about 2–10 amps helps avoid overheating and extends life. Keep jumper cables from touching to prevent shorts, and follow the charger's polarity and connection sequence to avoid damaging the unit or the vehicle's electrical system.

Store and care for the battery to extend its life: keep it clean and dry, and maintain charge above 12.4 volts to prevent sulfation. If the vehicle will sit for more than two weeks, use a battery maintainer. Protect the unit from extreme heat by parking in shade when possible. Cold reduces capacity, so test the battery before winter with a load tester to ensure reliable starting in low temperatures.

Testing the battery, starter, and alternator narrows down electrical faults. Follow these steps.

Start with a digital multimeter to measure open-circuit voltage. To avoid a surface charge, switch the headlights on for 30–60 seconds, turn them off, and wait two minutes. A full charge registers about **12.6-12.8 V**; roughly **12.4 V ≈ 75%**, **12.2 V ≈ 50%**, and **12.0 V** signals a low charge that should be corrected before further checks.

Next, perform a conductance or load test using a dedicated tester. Apply the load specified by the device or about 50% of the unit's CCA rating. If it won't hold charge after a proper recharge, replacement is likely. For a cranking test, clip the meter across the terminals while cranking; voltage should not fall below **9.6 V at 70°F**. A large drop indicates a weak cell or excessive resistance in the starter circuit.

Check the charging system with the engine running at idle and no extra loads. Charging voltage normally sits between **13.8 and 14.7 V**; some AGM systems run slightly lower. With headlights, blower, and defogger on, it should stay above **13.5 V**. Readings above **15.0 V** suggest overcharging (often a bad voltage regulator); below **13.2 V** points to undercharging from the alternator drive or wiring.

Perform a ripple test by switching the meter to AC volts and measuring at the terminals; more than **0.5 V AC** indicates a faulty diode in the alternator. To assess starter draw, use a clamp ammeter on the positive cable: high current with slow cranking suggests a seized engine or failing starter, while low current with slow crank points to high resistance in cables or grounds.

For suspected parasitic drain, ensure the vehicle is fully off and modules have entered sleep (about *10–45 minutes*). Put an ammeter in series with the negative cable. Typical draw is **20-50 mA**; anything over **~100 mA** warrants investigation.

Pull fuses one at a time to isolate the circuit—common culprits are courtesy lights, aftermarket accessories, and stuck relays.

Do voltage-drop tests under load across cables and connections. Aim for about **0.2 V** on power leads and **0.1-0.2 V** on grounds; higher values mean cleaning or repair is needed. Quick symptom cues: lights that brighten with RPM may indicate an alternator or belt issue; a flickering charge warning light can signal a diode or belt problem; clicking without crank often means a weak cell or poor terminal contact; slow cranking when hot can be starter heat soak; and intermittent electronics frequently trace back to poor grounds or low system voltage.

Include simple diagrams showing meter lead placement, a fuse-pull flowchart for parasitic drains, alternator and starter layouts, voltage-drop paths, and a quick-reference voltage chart to streamline troubleshooting.

Chapter 7: Brake Inspection, Maintenance & Replacement

Safety should be the priority when maintaining your vehicle's brakes. Before any inspection or maintenance, park on level ground to prevent unexpected movement. Chock the wheels that remain on the ground for extra security. When lifting the vehicle, support it with jack stands—never rely only on a jack. Wear eye protection, gloves, and a dust mask to protect against brake dust, which can contain harmful particles. Instead of blowing dust away, use brake cleaner and damp towels to keep contaminants from becoming airborne.

Begin by slightly loosening the lug nuts while the vehicle is still on the ground to prevent the wheels from spinning. Then raise the vehicle with a hydraulic or mechanical jack and support it with jack stands rated for your vehicle's weight. Remove the wheels completely, noting tire rotation direction and the torque specifications (usually in foot-pounds) for reassembly so the tires return in the correct orientation and are fastened to the manufacturer's standard.

With the wheels removed, inspect the components visually before disassembly. Look through the caliper window to check the pads; replace them if the friction material measures under **3 mm**. Examine the rotor for grooves, heat spots (*blueing*), or rust ridges, which indicate wear or overheating. Spin the wheel and listen for scraping or grinding that could point to rotor or pad damage.

Next, inspect the hoses for cracks, bulges, or damp spots that might indicate a leak, which can lead to failure. Also check calipers, wheel cylinders, the master cylinder, and brake lines for leakage; even a small loss of fluid can compromise the system.

Don't overlook the parking brake. Verify the lever or pedal has firm travel and releases fully. Inspect cables for fraying or seizing, and confirm rear caliper levers return to their stops when released to avoid unintended engagement.

Checking fluid is vital. Inspect the reservoir level and color; healthy fluid is amber or clear. Dark or brown fluid may contain moisture or be aged, risking performance and corrosion. A falling level can indicate pad wear or a leak and requires prompt investigation.

Note how the pedal feels; it reveals system issues. A soft or spongy pedal usually means air or moisture in the lines; a low, sinking pedal suggests a leak or a failing master cylinder. A hard pedal can indicate a problem with the booster or vacuum. If the vehicle pulls to one side under braking, a sticking caliper or bad hose may be to blame. Pedal pulsation during braking often comes from a warped rotor or an out-of-round drum, causing uneven stopping. Squealing typically stems from wear indicators or glazed pads and signals replacement.

Routine maintenance includes cleaning caliper slides and pad abutments. Lubricate guide pins and contact points with high-temperature grease, avoiding the pad face and rotor. Torque caliper bracket bolts to the manufacturer's specs from the service manual. Confirm even pad wear and that hoses are untwisted after reassembly.

When replacing pads and rotors, start by loosening the caliper bolts with the correct socket to avoid stripping, then support the caliper with a hook or wire so the hose isn't stressed. Remove the old pads and any clips or shims, keeping track of their orientation. Use a wire brush to clean the caliper bracket of rust and debris so the new hardware seats properly.

Compress the piston evenly with a **C-clamp** or a **retracting tool**; open the reservoir cap first so fluid can return and keep a catch bottle ready for overflow. If the vehicle has an **electronic parking brake**, place it in service mode before retracting the piston to protect the system.

Measure rotor thickness with a micrometer and check runout with a dial indicator, comparing both to the service manual limits. Replace or have rotors machined if they're under the minimum, cracked, deeply grooved, or out of tolerance. Clean replacement rotors with brake cleaner to remove any protective coating. Reinstall pads and new hardware, applying a light smear of **high-temperature grease** to abutments and the pad backs only—do not contaminate friction surfaces. When the wheels go back on, torque the lug nuts to the specified value in a star pattern.

For drum brakes, back off the adjuster through the access slot if the drum won't slide off. Replace shoes, springs, and hold-downs as a kit, and photograph assemblies before disassembly to aid reinstallation. Check wheel cylinders for leaks and lubricate backing-plate contact points lightly. Adjust the shoes for a slight drag when the drum is turned by hand.

Use the **DOT-rated fluid** specified by the manufacturer and bench-bleed any new master cylinder before fitting. Bleed the system from the wheel farthest from the master cylinder toward the nearest (or follow the vehicle's procedure), using a pressure bleeder, vacuum tool, or a helper, and keep the reservoir topped off while you work. A firm pedal after bleeding indicates air has been expelled.

Seat new pads and rotors with several moderate stops—generally *6–10* from roughly *30–40 mph*—allowing cool-down between stops to prevent overheating. After service, monitor the fluid level and watch for uneven pad wear, dragging brakes, or unusual smells or discoloration that could indicate sticking components, leaks, or other faults needing prompt attention.

CHAPTER 8: 4 TIRE MAINTENANCE AND REPAIR PROJECTS

Checking Tire Pressure and TPMS Diagnostics

Materials and Tools

- Digital tire pressure gauge (accurate to ±0.5 psi, reads 0–100 psi)
- Air compressor with pressure regulator (capable of 30–50 psi output)
- Tire valve stem caps (set of 4, standard size)
- TPMS (Tire Pressure Monitoring System) scan tool compatible with your vehicle's make/model
- Owner's manual for your vehicle (for recommended tire pressures and TPMS reset procedures)
- Work gloves (nitrile or latex-coated for grip)
- Flashlight (LED, 100+ lumens for clear visibility)
- Notebook or smartphone (to record readings)

Step-by-step instructions

1. Ensure the vehicle is parked on a flat, level surface and the tires are cold (vehicle has been stationary for at least 3 hours or driven less than 1 mile)
2. Remove all four valve stem caps and place them in a secure spot to avoid loss
3. Press the digital tire pressure gauge firmly onto the first tire's valve stem until the hissing sound stops and the reading stabilizes (usually within 2 seconds)
4. Record the pressure reading to the nearest 0.5 psi; repeat for all four tires, including the spare if equipped
5. Compare each reading to the recommended cold tire pressure listed on the driver's door jamb sticker or in the owner's manual (typically 32–36 psi for passenger vehicles)
6. If any tire is underinflated, attach the air compressor hose to the valve stem, set the regulator to the recommended psi, and inflate in short bursts, checking pressure after each burst to avoid overinflation
7. If a tire is overinflated, press the valve stem core briefly with the gauge or a small tool to release air, then recheck pressure
8. Replace all valve stem caps securely to prevent dirt and moisture from entering
9. Turn the ignition key to the "ON" position (engine off) and observe the TPMS warning light on the dashboard; if illuminated, proceed with TPMS diagnostics
10. Connect the TPMS scan tool to the vehicle's OBD-II port (usually under the dashboard, left of the steering column)
11. Follow the scan tool prompts to read TPMS sensor data for each

wheel; note any sensor with low battery, signal loss, or pressure discrepancy

12. If the scan tool indicates a sensor fault, consult the owner's manual for sensor replacement or reset procedures; some vehicles require driving above 15 mph for 10 minutes to reset the system, while others need a manual reset via dashboard controls

13. After adjustments and diagnostics, drive the vehicle for at least 5 minutes and recheck the TPMS warning light; if it remains off, the system is functioning correctly

Illustrations and diagrams

Diagram of a tire cross-section showing valve stem location and proper gauge placement
Illustration of a digital tire pressure gauge in use, with display reading
TPMS dashboard warning light symbols and their meanings
OBD-II port location diagram for common vehicle models

Practical expert tips

Check tire pressure at least once a month and before long trips; temperature changes of 10°F can alter tire pressure by 1 psi
Always use a digital gauge for accuracy; pencil-style gauges can be off by 2–3 psi
Inspect valve stems for cracks or leaks by applying soapy water and watching for bubbles
If your vehicle has a direct TPMS, avoid using aftermarket valve stem caps with metal inserts, as they can corrode and seize onto the sensor
Record tire pressures in a log to spot slow leaks or recurring issues over time

Troubleshooting techniques

If the gauge reads zero or erratic values, check for a dead battery or debris in the gauge nozzle
If a tire consistently loses pressure, inspect for embedded nails, sidewall damage, or a faulty valve core
If the TPMS warning light flashes for 60–90 seconds and then stays on, this usually indicates a sensor malfunction rather than low pressure
If the scan tool cannot communicate with a sensor, try rotating the tire 180° and rescanning, as sensor signal can be blocked by metal components
If the TPMS system will not reset, verify all tires (including the spare) are at correct pressure and that no sensors are missing or damaged

Security and preventive maintenance

Replace valve stem caps after every check to prevent contamination and slow leaks
Inspect tires for uneven wear, bulges, or sidewall cracks during pressure checks
Replace TPMS sensor batteries every 5–7 years or as indicated by the scan tool
Store the digital gauge and scan tool in a dry, cool place to prevent corrosion and battery drain
Check the air compressor hose and fittings for leaks or cracks before each use to ensure accurate inflation

Measuring Tread Depth and Rotating Tires

Materials and Tools

- Tire tread depth gauge (digital or manual, measures 0–32/32 inch)
- Torque wrench (calibrated, 10–150 ft-lb range)
- 1/2-inch drive breaker bar (minimum 18-inch length for leverage)
- 1/2-inch drive socket set (17mm, 19mm, 21mm common for lug nuts)
- Floor jack (rated for at least 2 tons, with a low-profile design for most vehicles)
- Jack stands (set of 4, each rated for at least 2 tons)
- Wheel chocks (set of 2, heavy-duty rubber or metal)
- Work gloves (nitrile-coated for grip and protection)
- Chalk or tire marker (for labeling tire positions)
- Shop rags (lint-free, for cleaning wheel hubs and lug nuts)
- Owner's manual (for vehicle-specific torque specs and rotation pattern)
- Flashlight (LED, 200+ lumens for clear visibility)

Step-by-step instructions

1. Park the vehicle on a flat, level surface such as a concrete driveway or garage floor; engage the parking brake and place wheel chocks behind the rear tires if working on the front, or in front of the front tires if working on the rear
2. Consult the owner's manual for the recommended tire rotation pattern (front-wheel drive: typically front-to-rear, rearward cross; rear-wheel drive: rear-to-front, forward cross; all-wheel drive: X-pattern or as specified)
3. Loosen each lug nut on all four wheels by 1/2 turn using the breaker bar and correct socket, but do not remove them yet
4. Position the floor jack under the manufacturer's recommended lift point for the first corner; raise the vehicle until the tire is 2–3 inches off the ground
5. Place a jack stand under the vehicle at the designated support point; lower the jack until the vehicle rests securely on the stand; repeat for all four corners so the vehicle is fully supported
6. Remove the lug nuts and take off each wheel; use shop rags to wipe any dirt or debris from the wheel hub and lug nut threads
7. Use the tire tread depth gauge to measure tread at three points across each tire (outer, center, inner); insert the probe into the tread groove and press the base flat against the tire; record the reading in 32nds of an inch (replace tires at 2/32 inch or less, 4/32 inch for wet climates)
8. Inspect each tire for uneven wear, bulges, sidewall cracks, or embedded objects; note any abnormal wear patterns for possible alignment or suspension issues
9. Mark each tire with chalk or a tire

marker to indicate its original position (e.g., "LF" for left front, "RR" for right rear)
10. Move each tire to its new position according to the rotation pattern; align the wheel with the hub and hand-thread the lug nuts to avoid cross-threading
11. Tighten lug nuts in a star pattern by hand until snug; repeat for all wheels
12. Lower the vehicle one corner at a time using the floor jack; remove jack stands and bring the tire fully to the ground
13. Set the torque wrench to the manufacturer's specified torque (typically 80–100 ft-lb for passenger vehicles); tighten each lug nut in a star pattern to ensure even seating
14. Double-check all lug nuts for proper torque; recheck after driving 50–100 miles

Illustrations and diagrams

Diagram of a tire cross-section showing correct placement of the tread depth gauge probe
Chart of common tire rotation patterns for front-wheel, rear-wheel, and all-wheel drive vehicles
Illustration of a star pattern for tightening lug nuts
Diagram of jack and jack stand placement points for a typical sedan

Practical expert tips

Always measure tread depth at multiple points to catch uneven wear; a difference of more than 2/32 inch across the tread indicates alignment or inflation issues
Rotate tires every 5,000–7,500 miles or at every oil change for even wear and maximum lifespan
Use a digital tread depth gauge for more precise readings, especially if you drive in wet or snowy conditions
If you notice cupping, feathering, or excessive wear on one edge, schedule a wheel alignment before rotating
Marking the date and mileage on the tire sidewall with a paint marker helps track rotation intervals

Troubleshooting techniques

If a lug nut is seized, apply penetrating oil (such as PB Blaster) and allow 10–15 minutes before attempting removal; use a breaker bar for extra leverage
If the tread depth gauge sticks or gives inconsistent readings, clean the probe and ensure it is perpendicular to the tread surface
If a tire cannot be removed from the hub due to corrosion, tap the sidewall gently with a rubber mallet while pulling outward
If the vehicle rocks or shifts on jack stands, lower it immediately and reposition the stands on a more stable, level surface

Security and preventive maintenance

Always use jack stands; never rely solely on a floor jack to support the vehicle
Inspect lug nuts and studs for rust or damage; replace any that show signs of wear or stripping
Clean wheel hubs with a wire brush to prevent corrosion and ensure proper wheel seating
Store the tread depth gauge and torque wrench in a dry, protected area to maintain accuracy
Check tire pressure after rotation

and adjust to the recommended psi listed on the driver's door jamb

Puncture Repair: Plug and Patch Method

Materials and Tools

- Tire plug kit (includes T-handle reamer, T-handle plug insertion tool, rubber plug strips, rubber cement)
- Tire patch kit (includes self-vulcanizing patches, patch roller, vulcanizing cement)
- Air compressor or portable tire inflator (capable of 30–50 psi output)
- Spray bottle with soapy water (1 tablespoon dish soap per 16 oz water)
- Valve core removal tool (brass or steel, fits standard Schrader valves)
- Tire pressure gauge (digital, accurate to ±0.5 psi)
- Jack and jack stands (each rated for at least 2 tons)
- Lug wrench (fits your vehicle's lug nuts, typically 17mm, 19mm, or 21mm)
- Chalk or tire marker
- Utility knife (with new blade)
- Pliers (needle-nose, for removing debris)
- Shop rags (lint-free)
- Nitrile gloves (5–7 mil thickness for chemical resistance)
- Safety glasses (ANSI Z87.1 rated)

Step-by-step instructions

1. Park the vehicle on a flat, stable surface such as a concrete driveway; engage the parking brake and place wheel chocks behind the tires opposite the one being repaired
2. Loosen the lug nuts on the affected wheel by 1/2 turn using the lug wrench, but do not remove them yet
3. Position the jack under the manufacturer's recommended lift point nearest the punctured tire; raise the vehicle until the tire is 2–3 inches off the ground and secure with a jack stand
4. Remove the lug nuts and take off the wheel; lay it flat with the valve stem facing up
5. Inspect the tire tread and sidewall for embedded objects; use pliers to remove any nail, screw, or debris causing the puncture
6. Spray soapy water over the puncture area and watch for bubbles to confirm the exact leak location; mark the spot with chalk or a tire marker
7. Insert the T-handle reamer into the puncture hole; push and twist the tool in and out 5–6 times to clean and roughen the hole for better plug adhesion
8. Thread a rubber plug strip halfway through the eye of the T-handle plug insertion tool; apply a generous amount of rubber cement to the plug and the puncture hole
9. Push the plug insertion tool into the hole until only 1/2 inch of the plug remains visible; pull the tool straight out, leaving the plug in place

10. Trim excess plug material flush with the tread using a utility knife
11. Deflate the tire completely by removing the valve core with the removal tool; break the tire bead using a bead breaker or by carefully prying with a tire iron (if equipped), then separate the tire bead from the rim just enough to access the inner liner at the puncture site
12. Clean the inner liner around the puncture with a shop rag; scuff a 2-inch diameter area around the hole using the buffer tool from the patch kit
13. Apply vulcanizing cement to the scuffed area and allow it to dry until tacky (about 2–3 minutes)
14. Remove the backing from the self-vulcanizing patch; center the patch over the puncture and press firmly, using the patch roller to eliminate air bubbles and ensure full adhesion
15. Reinstall the tire bead onto the rim; use the air compressor to inflate the tire to 5 psi, then check the patch area for leaks with soapy water
16. If no bubbles appear, reinstall the valve core and inflate the tire to the manufacturer's recommended pressure (typically 32–36 psi)
17. Mount the wheel back onto the vehicle; hand-thread the lug nuts, lower the vehicle, and torque the lug nuts in a star pattern to the specified value (usually 80–100 ft-lb)
18. Recheck tire pressure with the digital gauge and adjust as needed

Illustrations and diagrams

Cross-section diagram of a tire showing puncture location, plug insertion, and patch placement
Step-by-step illustration of T-handle reamer and plug tool use
Diagram of patch application on the inner liner with patch roller
Lug nut tightening star pattern chart

Practical expert tips

Always repair punctures within the tread area; never attempt to plug or patch sidewall or shoulder damage
Use both plug and patch for maximum safety and durability; plugs alone are temporary, patches alone may not seal the tread hole
Mark the repair date and mileage on the tire sidewall with a paint marker for future reference
Allow at least 30 minutes for the patch to cure before reinstalling and inflating the tire fully
Carry a portable tire inflator and plug kit in your trunk for emergency roadside repairs

Troubleshooting techniques

If the plug pulls out during insertion, the hole may be too large; use two plugs side by side or consult a tire professional
If the patch does not adhere, ensure the inner liner is completely clean, dry, and properly scuffed before applying cement
If air bubbles persist after repair, repeat the soapy water test and reapply the patch if necessary
If the tire will not reseat on the rim, use a bead seater or apply a small amount of soapy water to the bead for lubrication

Security and preventive maintenance

Inspect repaired tires every 1,000 miles for signs of air loss or further damage

Never exceed 50 mph or drive more than 100 miles on a plug-only repair; always follow up with a full plug-and-patch repair as soon as possible
Replace tires with punctures larger than 1/4 inch in diameter or with damage to the sidewall or shoulder
Store plug and patch kits in a cool, dry place and check expiration dates on vulcanizing cement and patches
Always wear gloves and safety glasses when handling tire repair chemicals and tools

Mounting, Balancing, and Valve Stem Replacement

Materials and Tools

- New tire(s) (correct size and load rating for your vehicle, DOT-approved)
- Wheel(s) (clean, undamaged, correct size for tire)
- Valve stem(s) (snap-in rubber, TR413 for most passenger vehicles, or metal clamp-in for high-pressure applications)
- Valve core tool (brass or steel, fits standard Schrader valves)
- Tire mounting lubricant (non-petroleum, commercial-grade, 16 oz bottle)
- Bead breaker (manual or hydraulic, compatible with wheel size)
- Tire irons or mounting bars (set of 2, 18-24 inch length, rounded edges)
- Rim protectors (polyurethane, set of 2-4)
- Wheel balancer (bubble balancer for DIY, or electronic spin balancer)
- Wheel weights (clip-on or adhesive, 0.25-2 oz increments, zinc or steel)
- Air compressor (minimum 5 CFM at 90 psi, with pressure regulator)
- Tire inflator with built-in gauge (accurate to ±0.5 psi, 0-60 psi range)
- Torque wrench (10-150 ft-lb range, 1/2-inch drive)
- Lug wrench (fits your vehicle's lug nuts, typically 17mm, 19mm, or 21mm)
- Jack and jack stands (each rated for at least 2 tons)
- Wheel chocks (set of 2, heavy-duty rubber)
- Shop rags (lint-free)
- Nitrile gloves (5-7 mil thickness)
- Safety glasses (ANSI Z87.1 rated)
- Chalk or tire marker

Step-by-step instructions

1. Park the vehicle on a flat, stable surface such as a concrete garage floor; engage the parking brake and place wheel chocks behind the tires opposite the one being serviced
2. Loosen the lug nuts on the wheel by 1/2 turn using the lug wrench, but do not remove them yet
3. Position the jack under the manufacturer's recommended lift point nearest the wheel; raise the vehicle until the tire is 2-3 inches off the ground and secure with a jack stand
4. Remove the lug nuts and take off

the wheel; lay it flat with the valve stem facing up

5. Deflate the tire completely by removing the valve core with the valve core tool; set the core aside in a clean area

6. Place the bead breaker against the tire sidewall, 1 inch from the rim; apply steady pressure to break the bead, working around the circumference until the bead is fully separated on both sides

7. Insert rim protectors between the tire bead and rim to prevent scratching; use tire irons to pry the bead over the rim edge, starting opposite the valve stem and working in 6-inch increments until one side is free

8. Repeat the process to remove the second bead, fully separating the tire from the rim

9. Remove the old valve stem by pulling it out with pliers or a valve stem puller; clean the valve hole with a shop rag

10. Lubricate the new valve stem with tire mounting lubricant; insert it through the hole from inside the rim and pull it into place until fully seated (the base should be flush with the rim surface)

11. Inspect the inside of the tire and rim for debris, corrosion, or sharp edges; clean thoroughly with a shop rag

12. Apply tire mounting lubricant to both tire beads and the rim edge; align the tire with the rim, positioning the red or yellow dot (if present) next to the valve stem for optimal balance

13. Push the lower bead over the rim edge by hand as far as possible; use tire irons to finish seating the bead, working in small increments and keeping rim protectors in place

14. Repeat for the upper bead, ensuring the tire is evenly seated all around

15. Inflate the tire to 5–10 psi using the air compressor and inflator; check that both beads "pop" into place with an audible snap—if not, apply more lubricant and gently tap the sidewall with a rubber mallet

16. Reinstall the valve core using the valve core tool; inflate the tire to the manufacturer's recommended pressure (typically 32–36 psi for passenger vehicles)

17. Mount the wheel on a bubble balancer or electronic spin balancer; follow the balancer's instructions to identify heavy spots

18. Attach wheel weights to the rim at the indicated locations, starting with the smallest increment needed; recheck balance and adjust as necessary until the bubble is centered or the machine reads "zero"

19. Mark the balanced position with chalk or a tire marker for reference

20. Mount the wheel back onto the vehicle; hand-thread the lug nuts, lower the vehicle, and torque the lug nuts in a star pattern to the specified value (usually 80–100 ft-lb)

21. Recheck tire pressure with the inflator gauge and adjust as needed

Illustrations and diagrams

Cross-section diagram of a wheel and tire showing bead, rim, and valve stem positions
Step-by-step illustration of bead breaking and tire iron use with rim protectors
Diagram of valve stem installation and seating
Bubble balancer setup and wheel

weight placement chart
Star pattern chart for lug nut tightening

Practical expert tips

Always use fresh, high-quality tire mounting lubricant to prevent bead damage and ensure easy installation
Mark the valve stem location on the tire before removal to help align balance dots during remounting
Use adhesive wheel weights for alloy rims and clip-on weights for steel rims; clean the rim surface with isopropyl alcohol before applying adhesive weights
If the tire bead is stubborn, warm the tire in direct sunlight for 15–20 minutes to increase flexibility
Double-check that the valve stem is fully seated by pulling gently with pliers—if it moves, reseat it with more lubricant

Troubleshooting techniques

If the bead will not break, reposition the bead breaker and apply gradual, even pressure; avoid using excessive force that could bend the rim
If the tire will not seat and "pop" onto the rim, check for dry spots and reapply lubricant; inflate in short bursts and tap the sidewall with a rubber mallet
If air leaks persist at the valve stem, remove and reinstall the stem with additional lubricant, ensuring no debris is present in the hole
If the wheel remains out of balance after adding weights, remove all weights and start the balancing process from scratch, checking for bent rims or uneven tire wear

Security and preventive maintenance

Inspect valve stems for cracks or dry rot at every tire change; replace any that show signs of aging or damage
Store tire irons, bead breaker, and balancer in a dry, protected area to prevent rust and maintain tool accuracy
Check wheel weights for looseness or corrosion at every oil change; replace or reattach as needed
Always wear gloves and safety glasses when working with tire tools and compressed air
After mounting and balancing, drive 50–100 miles and recheck lug nut torque and tire pressure to ensure safety and performance

CHAPTER 4: TIRE MAINTENANCE AND REPAIR PROJECTS

Tire Inspection and Cleaning for Longevity

Materials and Tools

- Digital tire pressure gauge (accurate to ±0.5 psi, 0–60 psi range)

- Tread depth gauge (graduated in 1/32-inch increments)
- White tire chalk or tire marker
- Stiff-bristle tire brush (10-inch handle, nylon bristles)
- Soft-bristle wheel brush (for delicate wheel finishes)
- Bucket (at least 2 gallons capacity)
- pH-balanced car wash soap (16–32 oz, non-acidic, safe for rubber)
- Hose with adjustable spray nozzle (minimum 40 psi water pressure)
- Microfiber towels (16x16 inch, lint-free, set of 4)
- Tire protectant (water-based, UV-resistant, non-silicone, 16 oz)
- Nitrile gloves (5–7 mil thickness)
- Safety glasses (ANSI Z87.1 rated)
- Jack and jack stands (each rated for at least 2 tons, if rotating tires)
- Wheel chocks (set of 2, heavy-duty rubber)

Step-by-step instructions

1. Park the vehicle on a flat, paved surface such as a concrete driveway; engage the parking brake and place wheel chocks behind the rear tires if working on the front, or vice versa
2. Inspect each tire sidewall for cracks, bulges, or cuts; run your gloved hand along the sidewall and look for any raised areas or deep grooves—mark any damage with tire chalk for further evaluation
3. Check the tread depth at three points across each tire (outer, center, inner) using the tread depth gauge; insert the probe into the tread groove and record the measurement—replace tires with less than 2/32 inch tread remaining
4. Examine the tread for uneven wear patterns such as cupping, feathering, or bald spots; note any irregularities with a tire marker and compare across all four tires to identify alignment or suspension issues
5. Look for embedded objects (nails, screws, glass) in the tread; remove any debris with pliers and mark the location for possible repair
6. Check for signs of dry rot by gently flexing the sidewall and inspecting for fine cracks, especially near the bead and shoulder area
7. Measure tire pressure with the digital gauge when tires are cold (vehicle parked for at least 3 hours); compare each reading to the manufacturer's recommended pressure (usually found on the driver's door jamb sticker)—add or release air as needed to match the specified psi
8. Fill a bucket with 2 gallons of water and add 2 ounces of pH-balanced car wash soap; mix thoroughly to create suds
9. Rinse each tire and wheel with a strong stream of water from the hose to remove loose dirt and brake dust
10. Dip the stiff-bristle tire brush into the soapy water and scrub the tire sidewall and tread in a circular motion, focusing on raised letters and grooves; use the soft-bristle wheel brush for the wheel surface to avoid scratching
11. Rinse thoroughly with clean water, ensuring all soap residue is removed from both tire and wheel
12. Dry each tire and wheel with a clean microfiber towel, wiping in a circular motion to prevent water spots
13. Apply a thin, even coat of water-based tire protectant to the sidewall using a dedicated microfiber applicator pad; avoid getting

protectant on the tread surface to maintain traction

14. Allow the protectant to dry for at least 10 minutes before driving; repeat the process for all four tires

Illustrations and diagrams

Diagram of tire cross-section showing tread, sidewall, bead, and shoulder areas for inspection
Illustration of proper tread depth gauge placement at three points across the tire
Step-by-step visual of tire cleaning: brushing, rinsing, drying, and protectant application
Chart of common tread wear patterns and their causes (e.g., underinflation, misalignment)

Practical expert tips

Always check tire pressure when tires are cold for the most accurate reading; heat from driving can increase pressure by 2–4 psi
Rotate tires every 5,000–7,500 miles to promote even wear and extend tire life
Use a separate brush for tires and wheels to prevent cross-contamination of brake dust and road grime
Avoid petroleum-based tire dressings, which can degrade rubber and cause premature cracking
Mark the inspection date and mileage on the inside of the wheel with a paint marker for future reference

Troubleshooting techniques

If you notice rapid or uneven tread wear, check for suspension issues or improper wheel alignment and schedule a professional inspection

Persistent low tire pressure may indicate a slow leak; perform a soapy water test around the valve stem, bead, and tread to locate leaks
If the tire protectant leaves a greasy or streaky finish, use less product and buff with a dry microfiber towel to achieve an even appearance
If brake dust is difficult to remove, use a dedicated wheel cleaner (acid-free, pH-neutral) and allow it to dwell for 2–3 minutes before scrubbing

Security and preventive maintenance

Inspect tires for damage and check pressure at least once a month and before long trips
Store tire cleaning supplies in a cool, dry place away from direct sunlight to preserve their effectiveness
Replace tires immediately if you find sidewall bulges, deep cuts, or exposed cords during inspection
Always wear gloves and safety glasses when handling cleaning chemicals and tools
Keep a record of tire inspections, rotations, and cleanings in your vehicle maintenance log for reference and warranty purposes

Seasonal Tire Changeover and Proper Storage

THE CAR MAINTENANCE AND REPAIR BIBLE

Materials and Tools

- Full set of seasonal tires (all-season, summer, or winter, DOT-approved, correct size and load rating for your vehicle)
- Jack and jack stands (each rated for at least 2 tons)
- Lug wrench (fits your vehicle's lug nuts, typically 17mm, 19mm, or 21mm)
- Torque wrench (10–150 ft-lb range, 1/2-inch drive)
- Wheel chocks (set of 2, heavy-duty rubber)
- Digital tire pressure gauge (accurate to ±0.5 psi, 0–60 psi range)
- Tread depth gauge (graduated in 1/32-inch increments)
- Wire brush (8-inch handle, medium bristle, for cleaning hub faces)
- Anti-seize compound (nickel or copper-based, 1 oz tube)
- Chalk or tire marker
- Microfiber towels (16x16 inch, lint-free, set of 2)
- Heavy-duty plastic tire bags (minimum 4 mil thickness, one per tire)
- Tire storage stands or racks (steel or heavy-duty plastic, rated for at least 200 lbs)
- Nitrile gloves (5–7 mil thickness)
- Safety glasses (ANSI Z87.1 rated)
- Shop vacuum (for cleaning storage area)

Step-by-step instructions

1. Park the vehicle on a flat, paved surface such as a concrete garage floor; engage the parking brake and place wheel chocks behind the tires opposite the end being lifted
2. Loosen the lug nuts on all wheels by 1/2 turn using the lug wrench, but do not remove them yet
3. Position the jack under the manufacturer's recommended lift point for the first wheel; raise the vehicle until the tire is 2–3 inches off the ground and secure with a jack stand
4. Remove the lug nuts and take off the wheel; mark the position (e.g., "LF" for left front) on the tire sidewall with chalk or a tire marker for future reference
5. Inspect the removed tire for tread depth (replace if less than 2/32 inch), sidewall cracks, bulges, or embedded debris; record any issues for repair or replacement
6. Clean the wheel hub face and mounting surface with a wire brush to remove rust and debris; wipe with a microfiber towel
7. Apply a thin layer of anti-seize compound to the hub face (avoid getting any on the wheel studs or brake components)
8. Mount the seasonal tire onto the hub, aligning the bolt holes; hand-thread the lug nuts
9. Lower the vehicle and remove the jack stand; torque the lug nuts in a star pattern to the manufacturer's specified value (usually 80–100 ft-lb)
10. Repeat the process for all four wheels, working one wheel at a time

for maximum safety

11. Check the tire pressure of all installed tires with a digital gauge; adjust to the manufacturer's recommended psi (found on the driver's door jamb sticker)

12. After all tires are changed, drive the vehicle for 2-3 miles, then recheck and retorque all lug nuts to ensure proper seating

Proper Storage of Off-Season Tires

Clean each removed tire and wheel with water and a mild car wash soap; dry thoroughly with a microfiber towel

Place each tire in a heavy-duty plastic tire bag; remove as much air as possible and seal the bag with tape to reduce exposure to moisture and ozone

Store tires vertically (standing up) on a tire rack or stand in a cool, dry area away from direct sunlight, heat sources, and ozone-producing equipment (such as electric motors or furnaces)

Avoid stacking tires horizontally for long-term storage, as this can cause sidewall distortion; if stacking is unavoidable, stack no more than four high and rotate the stack monthly

Keep the storage area clean and free of chemicals, solvents, or petroleum products that could degrade rubber; use a shop vacuum to remove dust and debris before storing tires

Record the storage date and tire position on each bag for easy identification during the next changeover

Illustrations and diagrams

Diagram of proper jack and jack stand placement under vehicle lift points

Illustration of star pattern for lug nut tightening sequence

Cross-section diagram showing correct vertical tire storage on a rack versus improper horizontal stacking

Step-by-step visual of tire bagging and sealing process

Practical expert tips

Always change over all four tires at once to maintain balanced handling and traction, especially with AWD or 4WD vehicles

Mark each tire's previous position before removal to ensure even rotation and wear at the next installation

Inflate stored tires to 5 psi above normal to compensate for gradual air loss during storage, but never exceed the maximum pressure listed on the sidewall

If using alloy wheels, avoid storing them directly on concrete floors—place a piece of cardboard or wood under each tire to prevent moisture wicking and corrosion

Schedule seasonal tire changeovers when average daily temperatures consistently stay above 45°F (for summer tires) or below 45°F (for winter tires)

Troubleshooting techniques

If a wheel is stuck to the hub, tap the back of the tire with a rubber mallet in several spots to break the bond; avoid using metal tools that could damage the wheel

If lug nuts are difficult to remove, apply penetrating oil and allow it to soak for 10-15 minutes before

retrying

If you notice uneven tread wear on removed tires, check for alignment or suspension issues before reinstalling them next season

If tire bags develop condensation inside, open the bags briefly to air out and dry the tires before resealing

Security and preventive maintenance

Inspect all tires for damage, tread depth, and age (DOT date code) before each seasonal changeover; replace any tire older than 6 years or showing signs of dry rot

Store jack, stands, and tools in a dry, organized area to prevent rust and ensure readiness for future use

Always wear gloves and safety glasses when handling tires, wheels, and chemicals

Keep a detailed log of tire changeover dates, mileage, and storage conditions to track wear patterns and maximize tire lifespan

Locating and Repairing Slow Leaks and Bead Seals

Materials and Tools

- Spray bottle (16 oz, filled with water and 2 oz dish soap)
- Digital tire pressure gauge (accurate to ±0.5 psi, 0–60 psi range)
- Valve core tool (brass or steel, compatible with Schrader valves)
- Tire plug kit (includes T-handle reamer, plug insertion tool, rubber plugs, rubber cement)
- Bead sealer (non-flammable, brush-on, 8 oz can)
- Small wire brush (6-inch handle, medium bristle)
- Clean microfiber towels (16x16 inch, lint-free, set of 2)
- Air compressor (minimum 90 psi, with tire inflator attachment)
- Jack and jack stands (each rated for at least 2 tons)
- Wheel chocks (set of 2, heavy-duty rubber)
- Nitrile gloves (5–7 mil thickness)
- Safety glasses (ANSI Z87.1 rated)
- Chalk or tire marker
- Utility knife (with new blade)
- Bucket (for cleaning solution and rinsing)
- Torque wrench (10–150 ft-lb range, 1/2-inch drive)

Step-by-step instructions

1. Park the vehicle on a flat, paved surface such as a concrete driveway; engage the parking brake and place wheel chocks behind the tires opposite the end being lifted

2. Check tire pressure on all four tires using the digital gauge; record readings and compare to the manufacturer's recommended psi (found on the driver's door jamb sticker)

3. If a tire is consistently losing 2 psi or more per week, proceed to locate the leak

THE CAR MAINTENANCE AND REPAIR BIBLE

4. Inflate the suspect tire to 5 psi above the recommended pressure (do not exceed the maximum pressure listed on the sidewall)
5. Mix a solution of water and dish soap in the spray bottle (2 oz soap per 16 oz water); shake to create suds
6. Spray the soapy solution liberally over the entire tread area, sidewalls, valve stem, and around the bead (where the tire meets the rim)
7. Observe for bubbles forming and growing—mark any bubbling area with chalk or a tire marker; bubbling at the tread or sidewall indicates a puncture, at the valve stem indicates a faulty valve, and at the bead indicates a bead seal leak
8. For tread punctures less than 1/4 inch in diameter, use the tire plug kit: remove the object with pliers, insert the T-handle reamer into the hole and work it in and out to roughen and clean the puncture, coat a rubber plug with rubber cement, insert it halfway into the eye of the plug tool, push the plug into the hole until only 1/2 inch remains outside, then pull the tool straight out, leaving the plug in place; trim excess plug with a utility knife
9. For valve stem leaks, use the valve core tool to remove and replace the valve core; if leaking persists, replace the entire valve stem (requires tire removal and is best done at a tire shop)
10. For bead leaks, jack up the vehicle and secure with jack stands; remove the wheel and deflate the tire completely by pressing the valve core
11. Break the bead by pressing down on the tire sidewall with a bead breaker tool or by carefully using the vehicle's weight (place the tire flat under the car and lower the jack onto the sidewall, avoiding the rim)
12. Use the wire brush to clean the rim's bead seat and the corresponding area on the tire; remove all corrosion, dirt, and old sealer
13. Wipe both surfaces with a clean, damp microfiber towel and dry thoroughly
14. Apply a thin, even coat of bead sealer to the rim's bead seat using the included brush; avoid excess sealer, which can squeeze out and cause imbalance
15. Re-seat the bead by inflating the tire with the air compressor; listen for two loud pops as the bead seats on both sides
16. Inflate the tire to the recommended pressure, reinstall the wheel, and torque the lug nuts in a star pattern to the manufacturer's specified value (usually 80–100 ft-lb)
17. Recheck for leaks with the soapy solution; repeat the sealing process if bubbles persist

Illustrations and diagrams

Diagram of tire cross-section showing tread, sidewall, bead, and valve stem locations for leak detection
Step-by-step visual of soapy water leak test with bubble formation
Illustration of tire plug insertion process
Diagram of bead area cleaning and bead sealer application

Practical expert tips

Always check for leaks after any

repair by spraying the soapy solution and watching for new bubbles
Mark the leak location before removing the tire to avoid losing track of the problem area
Use only plugs for tread punctures; never attempt to plug sidewall or shoulder punctures—replace the tire instead
If a tire repeatedly loses air after bead sealing, inspect the rim for bends or cracks and have it professionally repaired or replaced
Store the tire plug kit and bead sealer in a cool, dry place to maintain their effectiveness

Troubleshooting techniques

If no bubbles appear but the tire still loses air, submerge the inflated tire in a large tub of water and watch for a slow stream of bubbles
If the bead will not re-seat with a standard air compressor, use a rapid air burst (from a tire shop) or a bead seating tool
If the plug does not stop the leak, remove and ream the hole again before inserting a new plug; persistent leaks may require a professional patch from inside the tire
If the valve stem continues to leak after core replacement, inspect for cracks or dry rot and replace the entire stem

Security and preventive maintenance

Inspect tire pressure and look for slow leaks at least once a month and before long trips
Replace tires with multiple plugs, sidewall damage, or persistent bead leaks to ensure safety
Always wear gloves and safety glasses when working with chemicals, compressed air, and sharp tools
Keep a log of all tire repairs, including date, location, and type of repair, for future reference and warranty claims

Safe Tire Removal and Full Replacement with a Spare

Materials and Tools

- Full-size or compact spare tire (inflated to 60 psi for compact, or manufacturer's spec for full-size; check DOT date code for age under 6 years)
- Scissor jack or hydraulic floor jack (minimum 2-ton capacity, with saddle width at least 3 inches)
- Jack handle or lug wrench (fits your vehicle's lug nuts, typically 17mm, 19mm, or 21mm)
- Torque wrench (10–150 ft-lb range, 1/2-inch drive)
- Wheel chocks (set of 2, heavy-duty rubber, at least 8 inches long)
- Nitrile gloves (5–7 mil thickness)
- Safety glasses (ANSI Z87.1 rated)
- Flashlight or headlamp (LED, 200+

lumens, for low-light conditions)
- Tire pressure gauge (digital, accurate to ±0.5 psi, 0–60 psi range)
- Microfiber towel (16x16 inch, lint-free)
- Vehicle owner's manual (for jack point reference)
- Reflective safety vest (ANSI/ISEA 107-2015 compliant)
- Warning triangle or road flares (DOT-approved, at least 15 minutes burn time for flares)
- Chalk or tire marker

Step-by-step instructions

1. Park the vehicle on a flat, paved surface such as a concrete shoulder or driveway; turn off the engine, engage the parking brake, and activate hazard lights
2. Place wheel chocks firmly against the tire diagonally opposite the flat (e.g., if changing right front, chock left rear)
3. Put on the reflective safety vest and set up a warning triangle or road flares at least 100 feet behind the vehicle if on a roadside
4. Retrieve the spare tire, jack, and tools from the trunk or undercarriage; inspect the spare for visible damage and check pressure with the gauge (inflate to 60 psi for compact, or as specified for full-size)
5. Loosen the lug nuts on the flat tire by 1/2 turn each using the lug wrench; do not remove them yet—work in a star pattern for 5-lug wheels or across from each other for 4-lug
6. Consult the owner's manual for the correct jack point nearest the flat tire; position the jack so the saddle contacts the reinforced pinch weld or frame rail, at least 6 inches inboard from the wheel edge
7. Raise the vehicle with the jack until the flat tire is 2–3 inches off the ground; ensure the jack is vertical and stable—never crawl under the vehicle
8. Remove the loosened lug nuts completely and place them in a clean area or inside a hubcap to prevent loss
9. Grasp the flat tire at the 3 and 9 o'clock positions; pull straight outward to remove it from the hub, using a gentle rocking motion if stuck
10. Inspect the hub face for rust or debris; wipe clean with a microfiber towel to ensure proper seating of the spare
11. Align the spare tire's bolt holes with the wheel studs; lift and slide the spare onto the hub, supporting its weight with your knees to avoid back strain
12. Hand-thread all lug nuts onto the studs, turning each 2–3 full turns to prevent cross-threading
13. Lower the vehicle slowly until the spare just contacts the ground and cannot spin; do not fully lower yet
14. Tighten the lug nuts in a star pattern (or across for 4-lug) using the lug wrench, applying moderate force
15. Fully lower the vehicle and remove the jack; torque the lug nuts to the manufacturer's specification (usually 80–100 ft-lb) using the torque wrench, again in a star pattern
16. Check the spare tire's pressure once more and adjust if necessary; stow the flat tire, jack, and tools securely in the trunk
17. Remove wheel chocks, warning triangle, and safety vest; drive no

faster than 50 mph on a compact spare and limit use to 50-70 miles until a full repair or replacement

Illustrations and diagrams

Diagram of correct jack and wheel chock placement relative to the vehicle
Illustration of star pattern for lug nut tightening sequence
Cross-section showing proper alignment of spare tire on wheel studs
Visual of warning triangle and safety vest use for roadside safety

Practical expert tips

Always check the spare's pressure monthly and before long trips; a flat spare is useless in emergencies
Mark the flat tire's position with chalk for later repair and to track recurring issues
If the wheel is stuck to the hub, tap the back of the tire with the heel of your hand or a rubber mallet—never use metal tools that could damage the wheel
Store a pair of disposable gloves and a microfiber towel with your spare kit to keep hands clean and improve grip
Practice a dry run of tire changes at home to build confidence and speed for real roadside situations

Troubleshooting techniques

If the jack sinks into soft ground, place a wide, flat board (at least 12x12 inches, 3/4-inch thick plywood) under the base for stability
If a lug nut is seized, apply penetrating oil and wait 10-15 minutes before retrying; use a breaker bar if available

If the spare will not fit, check for mismatched bolt patterns or obstructions on the hub; never force the wheel onto the studs
If the vehicle rocks or shifts on the jack, lower it immediately and reposition both jack and chocks before continuing

Security and preventive maintenance

Inspect the spare tire, jack, and tools every 3 months for corrosion, damage, or missing parts; replace as needed
Keep a log of tire changes, including date, mileage, and reason, to monitor tire wear and spot patterns
Always wear gloves and safety glasses to protect against sharp edges, debris, and chemical exposure
Store the spare in a cool, dry area of the trunk, away from direct sunlight and chemicals that could degrade rubber

CHAPTER 9: 4 FLUID CHECKS AND REPLACEMENT PROJECTS

Engine Oil Change and Filter Replacement

THE CAR MAINTENANCE AND REPAIR BIBLE

Materials and Tools

- Full-synthetic engine oil (SAE 5W-30, API SP, quantity per owner's manual, typically 4.5–6 quarts for most sedans)
- OEM or high-quality aftermarket oil filter (spin-on or cartridge type, matched to vehicle year/make/model)
- Oil filter wrench (strap, cap, or pliers type, sized for your filter)
- 3/8-inch drive ratchet and 6-inch extension
- Socket set (metric, typically 13mm or 15mm for drain plug)
- Oil drain pan (minimum 8-quart capacity, with anti-splash baffle)
- Funnel (wide-mouth, oil-resistant plastic, 6-inch diameter)
- Clean microfiber towels (16x16 inch, lint-free, set of 2)
- Nitrile gloves (5–7 mil thickness)
- Safety glasses (ANSI Z87.1 rated)
- Floor jack (minimum 2-ton capacity) and jack stands (pair, rated for at least 2 tons each)
- Wheel chocks (set of 2, heavy-duty rubber)
- New drain plug washer (aluminum or copper, matched to plug size)
- Torque wrench (10–80 ft-lb range, 3/8-inch drive)
- Shop light or headlamp (LED, 200+ lumens)
- Oil disposal container (approved, with secure lid, 5-gallon capacity)
- Vehicle owner's manual (for oil type, capacity, and filter location)

Step-by-step instructions

1. Park the vehicle on a flat, paved surface such as a concrete driveway; engage the parking brake and place wheel chocks behind the rear tires
2. Run the engine for 3–5 minutes to warm the oil to 100–120°F for better flow; shut off the engine and allow to cool for 2 minutes
3. Open the hood and remove the oil fill cap to allow air flow during draining
4. Raise the front of the vehicle using a floor jack at the manufacturer's recommended lift points; secure with jack stands placed under the frame rails at least 12 inches from the wheel wells
5. Position the oil drain pan directly under the oil pan drain plug; ensure the pan is offset to catch the initial oil stream
6. Put on nitrile gloves and safety glasses; use the correct socket and ratchet to loosen the drain plug counterclockwise; remove the plug by hand and let oil drain for 5–7 minutes until flow reduces to a drip
7. Inspect the drain plug for metal shavings; clean with a microfiber towel and replace the washer with a new one
8. Reinstall the drain plug by hand, then torque to the manufacturer's specification (typically 25–30 ft-lb for most sedans) using a torque wrench
9. Move the drain pan under the oil filter; use the oil filter wrench to loosen the filter counterclockwise; remove by hand, keeping the open

end upright to minimize spills
10. Check that the old filter's rubber gasket is not stuck to the engine mounting surface; wipe the surface clean with a microfiber towel
11. Apply a thin film of new engine oil to the gasket of the new filter; hand-thread the filter onto the mount until the gasket contacts the base, then tighten an additional 3/4 turn (spin-on) or as specified for cartridge types
12. Remove the jack stands and lower the vehicle to the ground
13. Insert the funnel into the oil fill port; pour in the specified amount of new oil (e.g., 4.5 quarts), pausing to check the dipstick after 4 quarts to avoid overfilling
14. Reinstall the oil fill cap securely; start the engine and let it idle for 1–2 minutes; check for leaks at the drain plug and filter
15. Shut off the engine and wait 3 minutes; check the oil level with the dipstick, adding oil in 4-ounce increments if below the "Full" mark
16. Wipe up any spilled oil with a microfiber towel; record the date, mileage, and oil type in your maintenance log
17. Pour used oil into the disposal container and take it to a recycling center or auto parts store

Illustrations and diagrams

Diagram of oil pan, drain plug, and filter location relative to engine and subframe
Cross-section of spin-on and cartridge oil filter types, showing gasket placement
Step-by-step visual of oil draining, filter removal, and new filter installation
Chart of torque values for common drain plug sizes

Practical expert tips

Always use a new drain plug washer to prevent slow leaks and ensure proper sealing
Pre-fill the new oil filter with fresh oil (if mounted vertically) to reduce dry start wear
Mark the date and mileage on the new filter with a permanent marker for easy tracking
Use a shop light to inspect for leaks after the engine runs; even a small drip can indicate a loose filter or plug
Keep a dedicated funnel for engine oil only to avoid contamination

Troubleshooting techniques

If the drain plug is seized, apply penetrating oil and wait 10 minutes before retrying; use a breaker bar if necessary
If the old filter gasket is stuck to the engine, carefully remove it with a plastic scraper to avoid damaging the sealing surface
If oil pressure warning light stays on after refill, shut off the engine immediately and check for low oil level or leaks
If the filter leaks after installation, remove and inspect for double gaskets or cross-threading; replace if necessary

Security and preventive maintenance

Change engine oil and filter every 5,000–7,500 miles or as specified in the owner's manual, using the correct oil grade and filter type
Inspect for oil leaks monthly and

after every oil change, especially around the drain plug and filter
Always wear gloves and safety glasses to protect against hot oil and debris
Store used oil in a sealed, labeled container away from children and pets until proper disposal

Coolant System Flush and Refill

Materials and Tools

- Pre-mixed 50/50 extended-life coolant (silicate-free, phosphate-free, compatible with aluminum radiators; quantity per owner's manual, typically 1.5–2.5 gallons for most sedans)
- Distilled water (1 gallon, for rinsing and topping off)
- Radiator flush solution (alkaline-based, 12–16 oz bottle, e.g., Prestone or Peak)
- Large drain pan (minimum 3-gallon capacity, chemical-resistant plastic)
- Funnel (wide-mouth, coolant-safe, 6-inch diameter)
- Nitrile gloves (5–7 mil thickness)
- Safety glasses (ANSI Z87.1 rated)
- Shop towels or microfiber cloths (16x16 inch, lint-free, set of 3)
- Flathead screwdriver (for hose clamps, 1/4-inch tip)
- Pliers (for spring-type hose clamps, 6–8 inch)
- 3/8-inch drive ratchet and socket set (metric, typically 10mm or 12mm for drain plug)
- Floor jack (minimum 2-ton capacity) and jack stands (pair, rated for at least 2 tons each)
- Wheel chocks (set of 2, heavy-duty rubber)
- Catch bottle or turkey baster (for reservoir extraction, 12–16 oz capacity)
- Vehicle owner's manual (for coolant type, capacity, and drain locations)
- Infrared thermometer (optional, -58°F to 1022°F range, for checking engine temperature)
- Coolant hydrometer or refractometer (for freeze point verification)
- Oil drain pan (for used coolant transport, with secure lid)
- Large plastic sheet or absorbent mat (to protect driveway, 3x5 feet minimum)

Step-by-step instructions

1. Park the vehicle on a flat, paved surface such as a concrete driveway; engage the parking brake and place wheel chocks behind the rear tires
2. Allow the engine to cool completely (at least 1 hour, or until the upper radiator hose is below 100°F as measured by infrared thermometer)
3. Open the hood and remove the radiator cap by pressing down and turning counterclockwise; if hot, use a shop towel and open slowly to release pressure
4. Place a large plastic sheet or

absorbent mat under the radiator and engine bay to catch spills
5. Position the drain pan directly under the radiator drain plug (petcock) or lower radiator hose connection
6. Use the correct socket or screwdriver to open the radiator drain plug 2-3 turns; if no drain plug, use pliers to loosen the lower radiator hose clamp and carefully twist off the hose to drain coolant
7. Allow coolant to drain fully (5-10 minutes); use a turkey baster to extract coolant from the overflow reservoir if not draining by gravity
8. Close the drain plug or reattach the lower hose securely; tighten hose clamps to manufacturer's torque (typically 30-40 in-lb for worm gear clamps)
9. Pour the radiator flush solution into the radiator using a funnel; fill the rest of the system with distilled water until the radiator is full
10. Reinstall the radiator cap and start the engine; set the heater to maximum hot and fan to high to circulate flush through the heater core
11. Run the engine at idle for 10-15 minutes or as specified on the flush product label; monitor temperature gauge to ensure it stays in the normal range
12. Shut off the engine and allow to cool completely (at least 30 minutes)
13. Remove the radiator cap and drain the system again into the pan; repeat the drain and fill process with distilled water until the drained water runs clear (usually 2-3 cycles)
14. After final rinse, close the drain plug or reattach the lower hose; ensure all clamps and plugs are tight and leak-free
15. Using a funnel, slowly fill the radiator with pre-mixed 50/50 coolant until full; fill the overflow reservoir to the "Full" or "Max" line
16. Start the engine and let it idle with the radiator cap off; watch for air bubbles escaping as the thermostat opens (usually after 5-10 minutes, when the upper hose becomes hot)
17. Add coolant as needed to keep the radiator full; once bubbling stops and the level stabilizes, reinstall the radiator cap securely
18. Check the overflow reservoir and top off to the "Full" line if needed
19. Wipe up any spilled coolant with shop towels; rinse the area with water to prevent pet or wildlife exposure
20. Dispose of used coolant and flush water at a certified recycling center or auto parts store; never pour down drains or onto the ground

Illustrations and diagrams

Diagram of radiator, drain plug, lower hose, and overflow reservoir locations relative to engine bay
Cross-section showing coolant flow path through radiator, engine block, and heater core
Step-by-step visual of drain, flush, and refill process with arrows indicating fluid movement
Chart of typical coolant capacities and freeze point readings for common vehicle types

Practical expert tips

Always use pre-mixed coolant or mix concentrate with distilled water (never tap water) to prevent mineral deposits and corrosion

Mark the date and mileage of the flush on a sticker under the hood for easy tracking

If the radiator cap gasket is cracked or brittle, replace it with a new cap rated to the correct pressure (typically 13–16 psi for most sedans)

Use a coolant hydrometer or refractometer to verify freeze protection to at least -34°F for most U.S. climates

Run the heater during the flush and refill to ensure complete coolant exchange in the heater core

Troubleshooting techniques

If coolant drains slowly, check for a clogged drain plug or hose; use a flexible brush or compressed air to clear obstructions

If the engine overheats after refill, check for trapped air by squeezing the upper radiator hose and "burping" the system with the cap off

If leaks are found at hose connections, retighten clamps or replace hoses showing cracks or bulges

If the coolant remains rusty or discolored after multiple flushes, consider a professional power flush or inspect for internal corrosion

Security and preventive maintenance

Inspect coolant level and condition monthly; top off only with the same type of coolant already in the system

Replace coolant every 5 years or 100,000 miles, or as specified in the owner's manual

Check all hoses for softness, swelling, or leaks at every oil change; replace as needed

Store unused coolant in a sealed, labeled container out of reach of children and pets

Always wear gloves and safety glasses to protect against chemical burns and splashes

Brake Fluid Inspection and Replacement

Materials and Tools

- DOT 3 or DOT 4 brake fluid (as specified in owner's manual, typically 1–2 quarts for a full flush)
- Brake bleeder kit (hand vacuum pump with reservoir, or one-way bleeder bottle, 16–20 oz capacity)
- Clear vinyl tubing (3/16-inch inner diameter, 24-inch length)
- Box-end wrench (typically 8mm or 10mm, matched to bleeder screw size)
- Turkey baster or fluid syringe (8–12 oz capacity, for reservoir extraction)
- Clean microfiber towels (16x16 inch, lint-free, set of 3)
- Nitrile gloves (5–7 mil thickness)
- Safety glasses (ANSI Z87.1 rated)
- Jack and jack stands (minimum 2-ton capacity, pair rated for at least 2 tons each)

- Wheel chocks (set of 2, heavy-duty rubber)
- Shop light or headlamp (LED, 200+ lumens)
- Brake cleaner spray (chlorinated or non-chlorinated, 14–16 oz can)
- Small wire brush (6-inch, brass bristles)
- Torque wrench (5–30 ft-lb range, 3/8-inch drive)
- Vehicle owner's manual (for fluid type, bleeding sequence, and torque specs)
- Disposable catch container (minimum 1-quart, chemical-resistant plastic, with secure lid)
- Masking tape and permanent marker (for labeling old/new fluid)

Step-by-step instructions

1. Park the vehicle on a flat, paved surface such as a concrete driveway; engage the parking brake and place wheel chocks behind the rear tires
2. Open the hood and locate the brake master cylinder reservoir (typically on the driver's side firewall, translucent plastic with "MIN" and "MAX" marks)
3. Clean the reservoir cap and surrounding area thoroughly with a microfiber towel and brake cleaner to prevent contamination
4. Remove the reservoir cap; use a turkey baster or fluid syringe to extract as much old brake fluid as possible, depositing it into a labeled disposable container
5. Wipe the inside of the reservoir with a clean towel if accessible; avoid introducing lint or debris
6. Fill the reservoir to the "MAX" line with fresh DOT 3 or DOT 4 brake fluid, using a funnel if needed
7. Raise the vehicle using a jack at the manufacturer's recommended lift points; secure with jack stands under the frame rails at least 12 inches from the wheel wells
8. Remove all four wheels using a lug wrench or impact driver (typically 19mm or 21mm socket)
9. Starting with the wheel farthest from the master cylinder (usually right rear), locate the brake caliper or wheel cylinder bleeder screw; clean the area with brake cleaner and a wire brush
10. Attach a clear vinyl tube to the bleeder screw nipple; place the other end into a catch bottle partially filled with fresh brake fluid to submerge the tube tip
11. Use the correct box-end wrench to loosen the bleeder screw 1/4 turn; have an assistant slowly press the brake pedal to the floor and hold
12. Observe fluid flow through the tube; when pedal is held, tighten the bleeder screw, then instruct the assistant to release the pedal
13. Repeat the press-hold-open-close-release cycle, adding fresh fluid to the reservoir as needed to prevent it from dropping below the "MIN" line (check after every 3–4 cycles)
14. Continue until clear, bubble-free fluid emerges from the tube (typically 6–10 pedal cycles per wheel)
15. Tighten the bleeder screw to the manufacturer's torque specification (usually 6–10 ft-lb); remove the tube and wipe the area clean
16. Repeat the bleeding process for the next farthest wheel (left rear, right front, left front), following the correct sequence for your vehicle
17. After all wheels are bled, top off the reservoir to the "MAX" line and reinstall the cap securely

18. Reinstall all wheels; torque lug nuts to manufacturer's specification (typically 80–100 ft-lb for most sedans) using a torque wrench
19. Lower the vehicle to the ground; remove jack stands and wheel chocks
20. Pump the brake pedal several times until it feels firm; check for leaks at all bleeder screws and around the master cylinder
21. Dispose of old brake fluid at a certified recycling center or auto parts store; never pour down drains or onto the ground

Illustrations and diagrams

Diagram of brake master cylinder reservoir location and fluid level markings
Schematic of brake system layout showing correct bleeding sequence (e.g., RR, LR, RF, LF)
Cross-section of caliper/wheel cylinder with bleeder screw and tubing attachment
Step-by-step visual of pedal press, bleeder open/close, and fluid flow through clear tubing

Practical expert tips

Always use brake fluid from a sealed container; brake fluid absorbs moisture from the air, reducing effectiveness
Label old and new fluid containers clearly to avoid accidental reuse
If working alone, use a one-way bleeder bottle or hand vacuum pump to draw fluid without pedal assistance
Place a shop light under the vehicle to easily spot leaks during and after bleeding
Mark the date and mileage of the fluid change on a sticker under the hood for future reference

Troubleshooting techniques

If the brake pedal feels spongy after bleeding, repeat the process to remove trapped air; check for leaks at all connections
If a bleeder screw is seized, apply penetrating oil and wait 10 minutes; gently tap with a small hammer before retrying
If fluid drains slowly, check for clogged bleeder screws or collapsed rubber brake hoses
If the reservoir empties during bleeding, air may enter the system; restart the bleeding process from the beginning

Security and preventive maintenance

Inspect brake fluid level and color monthly; fluid should be clear to light amber, never dark brown or black
Replace brake fluid every 2 years or 24,000 miles, or as specified in the owner's manual
Always wear gloves and safety glasses to protect against corrosive brake fluid
Immediately rinse any brake fluid spills from painted surfaces with water to prevent damage
Check for leaks at the master cylinder, calipers, and wheel cylinders after every fluid change and at every oil change

Automatic Transmission Fluid Check and Service

Materials and Tools

- Automatic transmission fluid (ATF) type and quantity as specified in owner's manual (typically 4–12 quarts for a full service; e.g., Dexron VI, Mercon V, ATF+4)
- Transmission fluid filter kit (includes filter, pan gasket, and O-rings, matched to vehicle make/model/year)
- 3/8-inch drive ratchet and socket set (metric and SAE, typically 8mm–13mm for pan bolts)
- Torque wrench (5–20 ft-lb range, 3/8-inch drive)
- Large drain pan (minimum 2-gallon capacity, chemical-resistant plastic)
- Funnel with long, flexible neck (ATF-compatible, 1-inch diameter)
- Clean microfiber towels (16x16 inch, lint-free, set of 3)
- Nitrile gloves (5–7 mil thickness)
- Safety glasses (ANSI Z87.1 rated)
- Floor jack (minimum 2-ton capacity) and jack stands (pair, rated for at least 2 tons each)
- Wheel chocks (set of 2, heavy-duty rubber)
- Flathead screwdriver (for prying pan, 1/4-inch tip)
- Plastic scraper (for gasket removal, 1-inch wide)
- Brake cleaner spray (chlorinated or non-chlorinated, 14–16 oz can)
- Shop light or headlamp (LED, 200+ lumens)
- Disposable catch container (minimum 2-gallon, with secure lid, for used ATF)
- Vehicle owner's manual (for fluid type, fill/check procedure, and torque specs)
- Infrared thermometer (optional, -58°F to 1022°F range, for checking fluid temperature)
- New transmission pan bolts (optional, if originals are corroded or damaged)

Step-by-step instructions

1. Park the vehicle on a flat, paved surface such as a concrete driveway; engage the parking brake and place wheel chocks behind the rear tires
2. Start the engine and let it idle for 5–10 minutes to bring the transmission fluid to operating temperature (typically 150–200°F); shift through all gears with foot on brake, then return to Park
3. Shut off the engine; open the hood and locate the transmission dipstick (usually labeled "ATF" or "Transmission" near the engine bay firewall)
4. With the engine idling and transmission in Park, pull the dipstick, wipe clean with a microfiber towel, reinsert fully, then remove again to check fluid level and color; fluid should be between "MIN" and "MAX" marks and appear bright red or pink, not brown or burnt
5. If fluid is low, add ATF in 1/2-pint increments using a funnel; recheck level after each addition
6. To service the fluid, raise the vehicle using a floor jack at the

manufacturer's recommended lift points; secure with jack stands under the frame rails at least 12 inches from the wheel wells

7. Place a large drain pan under the transmission pan; use a ratchet and correct socket to loosen pan bolts in a crisscross pattern, leaving two bolts at opposite corners partially threaded to control pan drop

8. Carefully pry the pan loose with a flathead screwdriver, allowing fluid to drain into the pan; once most fluid has drained (3-5 minutes), remove remaining bolts and lower the pan completely

9. Remove the old transmission filter by unscrewing or unclipping it from the valve body; note orientation and O-ring placement

10. Install the new filter and O-ring from the kit, pressing firmly until fully seated; ensure no old gasket material remains on the mating surface

11. Clean the transmission pan thoroughly with brake cleaner and a microfiber towel; scrape off old gasket material with a plastic scraper, avoiding gouges

12. Place the new pan gasket onto the pan, aligning all bolt holes; position the pan against the transmission and hand-thread all bolts

13. Tighten pan bolts in a crisscross pattern to the manufacturer's torque specification (typically 8-12 ft-lb); do not overtighten to avoid warping the pan

14. Lower the vehicle to the ground; insert a funnel into the transmission dipstick tube and add the specified amount of new ATF (usually 3-5 quarts for a pan drop, or as specified in the manual)

15. Start the engine and let it idle; with foot on brake, shift through all gears for 2-3 seconds each, then return to Park

16. With engine idling, check the fluid level on the dipstick; add ATF in 1/2-pint increments until the level reaches the "MAX" mark

17. Inspect under the vehicle for leaks around the pan and gasket; wipe any drips with a towel

18. Dispose of used ATF and filter at a certified recycling center or auto parts store; never pour down drains or onto the ground

Illustrations and diagrams

Diagram of transmission dipstick location and fluid level markings
Cross-section of transmission pan, filter, and valve body assembly
Step-by-step visual of pan removal, filter replacement, and gasket installation
Chart of common ATF types and color/condition indicators

Practical expert tips

Always use the exact ATF type specified in your owner's manual; mixing types can cause shifting problems or transmission damage
Mark the date and mileage of the fluid change on a sticker under the hood or in your maintenance log
If the pan gasket is cork or rubber, lightly coat with ATF before installation to improve sealing
Use a shop light to inspect the old fluid for metal shavings or debris, which may indicate internal wear
If the transmission has a drain plug, use it to drain fluid before pan removal to minimize mess

Troubleshooting techniques

If fluid level drops after service, check for leaks at the pan gasket and drain plug; retighten bolts to spec if needed

If shifting becomes erratic after fluid change, verify correct ATF type and level; overfilling can cause foaming and slipping

If the dipstick shows milky or cloudy fluid, inspect for coolant contamination from a failed radiator transmission cooler

If the pan bolts strip or break, replace with new bolts of the correct grade and length

Security and preventive maintenance

Check transmission fluid level and color monthly; fluid should remain bright red and at the correct level

Replace ATF and filter every 30,000–60,000 miles, or as specified in the owner's manual

Inspect for leaks at the pan, cooler lines, and dipstick tube at every oil change

Always wear gloves and safety glasses to protect against hot fluid and chemical exposure

Store unused ATF in a sealed, labeled container out of reach of children and pets

4 FLUID CHECKS AND REPLACEMENT PROJECTS

Power Steering Fluid Inspection and Replacement

Materials and Tools

- Power steering fluid (type and quantity as specified in owner's manual, typically 1–2 quarts; e.g., Dexron III/Mercon, ATF+4, or manufacturer-specific)
- Turkey baster or fluid syringe (8–12 oz capacity, for reservoir extraction)
- Clean microfiber towels (16x16 inch, lint-free, set of 3)
- Nitrile gloves (5–7 mil thickness)
- Safety glasses (ANSI Z87.1 rated)
- Jack and jack stands (minimum 2-ton capacity, pair rated for at least 2 tons each)
- Wheel chocks (set of 2, heavy-duty rubber)
- Shop light or headlamp (LED, 200+ lumens)
- Disposable catch container (minimum 1-quart, chemical-resistant plastic, with secure lid)
- Small funnel (ATF-compatible, 1-inch diameter)
- Flathead screwdriver (for hose clamp removal, 1/4-inch tip)
- Pliers (for hose removal, 6–8 inch)
- Vehicle owner's manual (for fluid type, reservoir location, and capacity)
- Masking tape and permanent marker (for labeling old/new fluid)
- Brake cleaner spray (chlorinated or

non-chlorinated, 14–16 oz can)
- New power steering return hose clamps (optional, if originals are corroded or damaged)

Step-by-step instructions

1. Park the vehicle on a flat, paved surface such as a concrete driveway; engage the parking brake and place wheel chocks behind the rear tires
2. Open the hood and locate the power steering fluid reservoir (typically a round or rectangular translucent plastic or metal container near the engine, often labeled "Power Steering")
3. Clean the reservoir cap and surrounding area thoroughly with a microfiber towel and brake cleaner to prevent contamination
4. Remove the reservoir cap; check the fluid level against the "MIN" and "MAX" marks on the dipstick or reservoir body
5. Inspect fluid color and condition: fluid should be clear, red, or amber (depending on type), not dark brown, black, or milky
6. If fluid is low, add the specified power steering fluid in 2–4 oz increments using a funnel; recheck level after each addition
7. For a full fluid replacement, use a turkey baster or fluid syringe to extract as much old fluid as possible from the reservoir, depositing it into a labeled disposable container
8. Wipe the inside of the reservoir with a clean towel if accessible; avoid introducing lint or debris
9. Refill the reservoir to the "MAX" line with fresh power steering fluid
10. Raise the front of the vehicle using a jack at the manufacturer's recommended lift points; secure with jack stands under the frame rails at least 12 inches from the wheel wells
11. Place a catch container under the power steering return hose connection at the reservoir
12. Use pliers or a flathead screwdriver to loosen and remove the return hose clamp; carefully disconnect the hose and direct it into the catch container
13. Have an assistant start the engine and slowly turn the steering wheel from lock to lock (full left to full right) several times to flush old fluid from the system; add fresh fluid to the reservoir as it drains to prevent air from entering the system
14. Continue flushing until clean, new fluid flows from the return hose (typically 1–2 quarts total)
15. Reconnect the return hose and secure with the clamp; wipe any spilled fluid with a towel and brake cleaner
16. Lower the vehicle to the ground; top off the reservoir to the "MAX" line with fresh fluid
17. Start the engine and turn the steering wheel from lock to lock several times to purge air; check fluid level and add as needed
18. Inspect for leaks at the reservoir, hoses, and connections; wipe any drips with a towel
19. Dispose of old power steering fluid at a certified recycling center or auto parts store; never pour down drains or onto the ground

Illustrations and diagrams

Diagram of power steering fluid reservoir location and fluid level markings
Cross-section of reservoir showing dipstick, "MIN" and "MAX" lines, and fluid color examples

Schematic of power steering system with return hose and flush flow direction
Step-by-step visual of fluid extraction, hose removal, and fluid flush process

Practical expert tips

Always use the exact power steering fluid type specified in your owner's manual; mixing types can cause seal damage or steering noise
Mark the date and mileage of the fluid change on a sticker under the hood or in your maintenance log
If the reservoir has a filter screen, inspect and clean it with brake cleaner before refilling
Use a shop light to inspect hoses for cracks, bulges, or leaks during service
Replace old or corroded hose clamps to prevent future leaks

Troubleshooting techniques

If the steering feels stiff or noisy after service, check for low fluid level or trapped air; repeat the lock-to-lock steering process to purge air
If fluid foams or appears milky, inspect for air leaks at hose connections or possible water contamination
If the reservoir empties rapidly during flushing, add fluid continuously to prevent air from entering the system
If leaks persist after hose reconnection, inspect hose ends and clamps for damage; replace as needed

Security and preventive maintenance

Check power steering fluid level and color monthly; fluid should remain clear and at the correct level
Replace power steering fluid every 2 years or 24,000–30,000 miles, or as specified in the owner's manual
Inspect hoses and clamps for leaks, cracks, or wear at every oil change
Always wear gloves and safety glasses to protect against fluid splashes and chemical exposure
Immediately rinse any power steering fluid spills from painted surfaces with water to prevent damage

Rear Differential Fluid Change and Seal Inspection

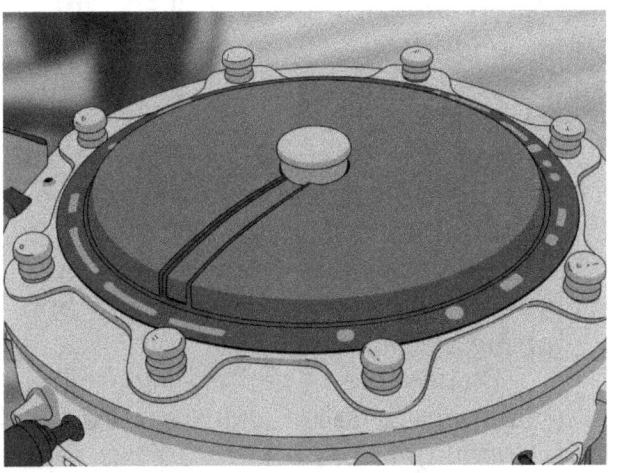

Materials and Tools

- Rear differential fluid (type and quantity as specified in owner's manual, typically 1.5–3 quarts; e.g., 75W-90 or 80W-90 GL-5 gear oil, synthetic or conventional)
- New differential cover gasket or RTV silicone gasket maker (oil-resistant, gray or black, 3 oz tube)
- 3/8-inch drive ratchet and socket set (metric and SAE, typically 10mm–14mm for cover bolts)
- Torque wrench (20–60 ft-lb range,

3/8-inch drive)
- Large drain pan (minimum 2-gallon capacity, chemical-resistant plastic)
- Gasket scraper or plastic putty knife (1-inch wide)
- Brake cleaner spray (chlorinated or non-chlorinated, 14–16 oz can)
- Clean microfiber towels (16x16 inch, lint-free, set of 3)
- Nitrile gloves (5–7 mil thickness)
- Safety glasses (ANSI Z87.1 rated)
- Floor jack (minimum 2-ton capacity) and jack stands (pair, rated for at least 2 tons each)
- Wheel chocks (set of 2, heavy-duty rubber)
- Fluid pump (manual or drill-operated, compatible with gear oil bottles)
- Shop light or headlamp (LED, 200+ lumens)
- Flathead screwdriver (for prying cover, 1/4-inch tip)
- New differential cover bolts (optional, if originals are corroded or damaged)
- Vehicle owner's manual (for fluid type, fill/check procedure, and torque specs)
- Disposable catch container (minimum 2-gallon, with secure lid, for used gear oil)
- Infrared thermometer (optional, -58°F to 1022°F range, for checking housing temperature)
- Thread locker (medium strength, blue, 0.2 oz tube, optional for bolts)

Step-by-step instructions

1. Park the vehicle on a flat, paved surface such as a concrete driveway; engage the parking brake and place wheel chocks in front of the front tires
2. Raise the rear of the vehicle using a floor jack at the manufacturer's recommended lift points; secure with jack stands under the axle tubes at least 12 inches from the wheel hubs
3. Place a large drain pan directly under the rear differential cover; use a shop light to illuminate the work area
4. Locate the differential fill plug (usually on the rear or side of the differential housing, 3/8-inch square drive or hex bolt); remove the fill plug first to ensure it can be opened before draining
5. Use a ratchet and correct socket to loosen and remove all but the top two differential cover bolts; leave the top bolts partially threaded to control the cover drop
6. Carefully pry the bottom of the cover loose with a flathead screwdriver, allowing old gear oil to drain into the pan; once most fluid has drained (3–5 minutes), remove the remaining bolts and lower the cover completely
7. Inspect the old fluid for metal shavings or debris; note any excessive glitter or chunks, which may indicate internal wear
8. Use a gasket scraper or plastic putty knife to remove all old gasket material from the cover and housing mating surfaces; avoid gouging the metal
9. Spray the inside of the housing and cover with brake cleaner; wipe thoroughly with microfiber towels until all residue and debris are removed
10. Inspect the pinion seal (where the driveshaft enters the differential) and axle seals (at each axle tube end) for signs of leaks: look for wetness, oil trails, or dirt accumulation around the seals

11. If any seal shows signs of leakage, note the location for future replacement; do not proceed with fluid refill if a major leak is present—schedule seal replacement first

12. If using a new gasket, align it with the bolt holes on the cover; if using RTV silicone, apply a continuous 1/8-inch bead around the cover's perimeter, encircling all bolt holes, and allow to skin for 10–15 minutes

13. Position the cover against the housing and hand-thread all bolts; tighten bolts in a crisscross pattern to the manufacturer's torque specification (typically 25–35 ft-lb); do not overtighten to avoid warping the cover

14. Insert the fluid pump into the gear oil bottle; pump new differential fluid into the fill hole until fluid begins to seep out of the opening (housing should be level for accurate fill)

15. Reinstall the fill plug and tighten to the specified torque (typically 20–30 ft-lb); wipe any excess oil from the housing

16. Lower the vehicle to the ground; clean up any spilled fluid with brake cleaner and towels

17. Dispose of used gear oil at a certified recycling center or auto parts store; never pour down drains or onto the ground

Illustrations and diagrams

Diagram of rear differential housing with fill and drain plug locations
Cross-section of differential showing cover, gasket, and fluid level
Step-by-step visual of cover removal, gasket installation, and fluid refill process
Schematic highlighting pinion and axle seal inspection points

Practical expert tips

Always use the exact gear oil type and viscosity specified in your owner's manual; incorrect fluid can cause gear whine or premature wear
Mark the date and mileage of the fluid change on a sticker on the differential cover or in your maintenance log
If the cover bolts are corroded or damaged, replace with new bolts and apply medium-strength thread locker to prevent loosening
Use a shop light to inspect the inside of the housing for pitting, scoring, or discoloration on the gears
If the fill plug is stuck, apply penetrating oil and use a breaker bar for extra leverage; never attempt to drain the fluid until the fill plug is confirmed removable

Troubleshooting techniques

If fluid leaks after service, check the cover bolts for proper torque and inspect the gasket or RTV bead for gaps or misalignment
If a whining or grinding noise develops after fluid change, verify correct fluid type and level; check for signs of internal wear in the old fluid
If the fill plug strips or breaks, replace with a new plug of the correct thread and size; avoid overtightening
If the cover warps during installation, remove and flatten on a hard surface or replace with a new cover

Security and preventive maintenance

Check rear differential fluid level and condition every 15,000 miles or annually; fluid should remain clear and at the correct level

Replace differential fluid every 30,000–60,000 miles, or as specified in the owner's manual, especially if towing or driving in severe conditions

Inspect pinion and axle seals for leaks at every oil change; address any leaks promptly to prevent gear damage

Always wear gloves and safety glasses to protect against hot fluid and chemical exposure

Store unused gear oil in a sealed, labeled container out of reach of children and pets

Transfer Case Fluid Check and Replacement

Materials and Tools

- Transfer case fluid (type and quantity as specified in owner's manual, typically 1.5–2.5 quarts; e.g., ATF+4, Dexron III/Mercon, or manufacturer-specific transfer case fluid)
- 3/8-inch drive ratchet and socket set (metric and SAE, typically 10mm–18mm for fill/drain plugs)
- Fluid pump (manual or drill-operated, compatible with transfer case fluid bottles)
- Large drain pan (minimum 2-gallon capacity, chemical-resistant plastic)
- Clean microfiber towels (16x16 inch, lint-free, set of 3)
- Nitrile gloves (5–7 mil thickness)
- Safety glasses (ANSI Z87.1 rated)
- Floor jack (minimum 2-ton capacity) and jack stands (pair, rated for at least 2 tons each)
- Wheel chocks (set of 2, heavy-duty rubber)
- Shop light or headlamp (LED, 200+ lumens)
- Flathead screwdriver (for prying stubborn plugs, 1/4-inch tip)
- New transfer case fill/drain plug washers (optional, if originals are damaged or leaking)
- Vehicle owner's manual (for fluid type, fill/check procedure, and torque specs)
- Disposable catch container (minimum 2-gallon, with secure lid, for used fluid)
- Thread sealant or Teflon tape (optional, for plug threads if specified by manufacturer)
- Torque wrench (10–40 ft-lb range, 3/8-inch drive)

Step-by-step instructions

1. Park the vehicle on a flat, paved surface such as a concrete driveway; engage the parking brake and place wheel chocks behind the rear tires
2. Raise the vehicle using a floor jack at the manufacturer's recommended lift points; secure with jack stands under the frame rails or axle tubes at least 12 inches from the wheel wells
3. Position a large drain pan directly

under the transfer case; use a shop light to illuminate the area
4. Locate the transfer case fill and drain plugs (typically on the rear or side of the transfer case; fill plug is higher, drain plug is lower)
5. Remove the fill plug first using a 3/8-inch drive ratchet and correct socket; this ensures the fill plug can be removed before draining fluid
6. Remove the drain plug and allow old fluid to drain completely into the pan (typically 5–10 minutes); inspect the fluid for metal shavings or discoloration
7. Clean both plugs thoroughly with a microfiber towel; inspect for damaged threads or worn sealing washers and replace if necessary
8. If required, apply thread sealant or Teflon tape to the plug threads as specified in the owner's manual
9. Reinstall the drain plug and tighten to the manufacturer's torque specification (typically 15–30 ft-lb); do not overtighten to avoid stripping threads
10. Insert the fluid pump into the new transfer case fluid bottle; pump fresh fluid into the fill hole until fluid begins to seep out of the opening (vehicle must be level for accurate fill)
11. Reinstall the fill plug and tighten to the specified torque (typically 15–30 ft-lb); wipe any excess fluid from the case with a towel
12. Lower the vehicle to the ground; clean up any spilled fluid with brake cleaner and towels
13. Dispose of used transfer case fluid at a certified recycling center or auto parts store; never pour down drains or onto the ground

Illustrations and diagrams

Diagram of transfer case location with fill and drain plug positions
Cross-section of transfer case showing fluid level and internal components
Step-by-step visual of plug removal, fluid drain, and refill process
Schematic highlighting correct fluid fill level and overflow point

Practical expert tips

Always use the exact transfer case fluid type and quantity specified in your owner's manual; incorrect fluid can cause shifting issues or internal damage
Mark the date and mileage of the fluid change on a sticker on the transfer case or in your maintenance log
If the fill or drain plug is stuck, apply penetrating oil and use a breaker bar for extra leverage; avoid using excessive force to prevent damage
Use a shop light to inspect the transfer case for leaks, cracks, or corrosion during service
Replace plug washers or gaskets if any seepage is observed after tightening

Troubleshooting techniques

If fluid leaks after service, check the plug torque and inspect washers or gaskets for proper sealing
If shifting problems or noise develop after fluid change, verify correct fluid type and level; check for signs of contamination in the old fluid
If the fill plug strips or breaks, replace with a new plug of the correct thread and size; avoid overtightening
If fluid overflows during filling, allow excess to drain until only a slow drip

remains, ensuring the correct level

Security and preventive maintenance

Check transfer case fluid level and condition every 15,000 miles or annually; fluid should remain clear and at the correct level
Replace transfer case fluid every 30,000–60,000 miles, or as specified in the owner's manual, especially if towing or driving in severe conditions
Inspect the transfer case and surrounding area for leaks at every oil change; address any leaks promptly to prevent drivetrain damage
Always wear gloves and safety glasses to protect against hot fluid and chemical exposure
Store unused transfer case fluid in a sealed, labeled container out of reach of children and pets

Windshield Washer System Flush, Nozzle Cleaning, and Refill

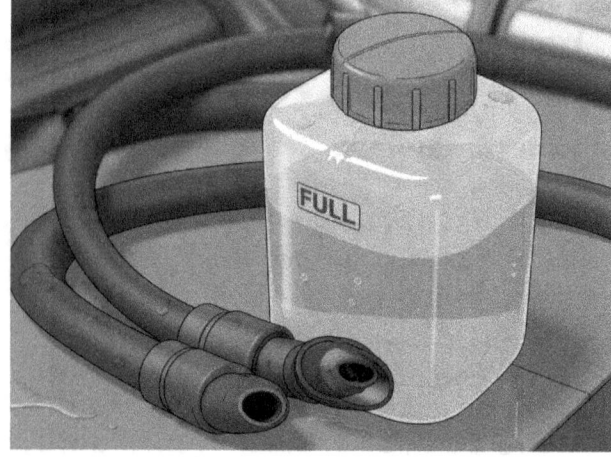

Materials and Tools

- Windshield washer fluid (pre-mixed, freeze protection to -20°F or lower, minimum 1 gallon; avoid plain water)
- Distilled water (1 quart, for flushing if needed)
- 10mm socket and ratchet (for washer reservoir removal, if required)
- Flathead screwdriver (1/4-inch tip, for prying hose clamps or covers)
- Needle or pin (stainless steel, 1–2 inches long, for nozzle cleaning)
- Compressed air canister (with straw nozzle, 8–12 oz)
- Clean microfiber towels (16x16 inch, lint-free, set of 2)
- Small funnel (2–3 inch diameter, chemical-resistant plastic)
- Nitrile gloves (5–7 mil thickness)
- Safety glasses (ANSI Z87.1 rated)
- Shop light or headlamp (LED, 200+ lumens)
- Catch pan or bucket (1–2 gallon, for old fluid)
- Turkey baster or fluid transfer syringe (8–12 oz capacity, for reservoir emptying)
- Owner's manual (for reservoir location and fluid type)
- Toothbrush (soft-bristled, for scrubbing nozzles and reservoir cap)
- Spray bottle (16 oz, filled with distilled water for rinsing)

Step-by-step instructions

1. Park the vehicle on a flat, paved surface; engage the parking brake and turn off the ignition
2. Open the hood and secure with the prop rod; use a shop light to illuminate the washer reservoir area
3. Locate the windshield washer fluid reservoir (typically a translucent plastic tank with a blue or black cap, marked with a windshield/water symbol)

4. Remove the reservoir cap; inspect for dirt or debris and clean with a microfiber towel and toothbrush
5. Use a turkey baster or fluid transfer syringe to remove as much old washer fluid as possible from the reservoir; transfer to a catch pan for disposal
6. If the reservoir is heavily contaminated (visible sediment, algae, or sludge), disconnect the washer hose at the base of the reservoir using a flathead screwdriver to loosen any hose clamp; direct the hose into a catch pan
7. Pour 1 quart of distilled water into the reservoir; allow it to drain through the disconnected hose to flush out remaining debris
8. Reconnect the washer hose securely; ensure the clamp is tight and the hose is fully seated
9. Fill the reservoir with 1 gallon of new windshield washer fluid using a funnel; avoid overfilling—stop when fluid reaches the "Full" line or is 1 inch below the fill neck
10. Replace the reservoir cap and wipe up any spills with a microfiber towel
11. Inspect washer nozzles (located on the hood or at the base of the windshield) for clogs or mineral buildup; use a needle or pin to gently clear each nozzle opening, inserting no more than 1/4 inch to avoid damage
12. Spray each nozzle with distilled water from a spray bottle; wipe clean with a towel
13. If spray pattern is weak or uneven, attach the straw nozzle to a compressed air canister and deliver a short burst (1–2 seconds) of air into each nozzle to clear internal blockages
14. Test the system by turning the ignition to "On" (engine off is acceptable) and activating the washer switch; observe spray pattern and coverage on the windshield
15. If any nozzle remains clogged, repeat cleaning and compressed air steps; if still blocked, inspect washer hoses for kinks or disconnections and repair as needed
16. Dispose of old washer fluid at a certified recycling center or auto parts store; never pour down drains or onto the ground

Illustrations and diagrams

Diagram of washer reservoir location and cap
Cross-section of washer nozzle showing internal passage and cleaning method
Schematic of washer hose routing from reservoir to nozzles
Step-by-step visual of reservoir draining, flushing, and refilling process

Practical expert tips

Always use washer fluid rated for your climate; in winter, select fluid with freeze protection to at least -20°F to prevent system damage
Mark the date and mileage of the flush and refill in your maintenance log or on a sticker near the reservoir
If you notice a vinegar or musty odor, add a washer fluid with a built-in mildew inhibitor to prevent algae growth
For stubborn nozzle clogs, soak the tip in a cup of warm distilled water for 10 minutes before cleaning with a pin

If the reservoir is difficult to access, consult your owner's manual for removal instructions or use a flexible funnel for easier filling

Troubleshooting techniques

If no fluid sprays after refill, check for a blown washer pump fuse (refer to fuse box diagram) and replace with the correct amperage fuse
If the washer pump runs but no fluid emerges, inspect for disconnected or kinked hoses between the reservoir and nozzles
If fluid leaks under the vehicle after filling, inspect the reservoir and hoses for cracks or loose connections; replace damaged parts as needed
If spray pattern is weak, verify the fluid level and check for partially clogged nozzles or low pump voltage (test with a multimeter, should be 12V at the pump connector)
If only one nozzle sprays, clean both nozzles and check the Y-connector or hose junction for blockages

Security and preventive maintenance

Check washer fluid level monthly and top off as needed, especially before long trips or during winter
Flush and refill the washer system every 12 months or at the start of each season for optimal performance
Inspect washer hoses and nozzles for leaks, cracks, or blockages at every oil change
Always wear gloves and safety glasses to protect against chemical exposure and accidental spray
Store unused washer fluid in a sealed, labeled container out of reach of children and pets

CHAPTER 10: LIGHTING AND ELECTRICAL FIX PROJECTS

Headlight Bulb Replacement and Beam Alignment

Materials and Tools

- Replacement headlight bulbs (halogen, HID, or LED; check owner's manual for correct type and wattage, e.g., H11 12V 55W halogen)
- Nitrile gloves (5–7 mil thickness, powder-free, size L)
- Clean microfiber towels (16x16 inch, lint-free, set of 2)
- Flathead screwdriver (1/4-inch tip, for prying retaining clips)
- Phillips screwdriver (#2, for headlight housing screws)
- 10mm socket and ratchet (for headlight assembly bolts)
- Dielectric grease (0.5 oz tube, for bulb terminals)
- Alcohol wipes (70% isopropyl, for cleaning bulb and housing)
- Tape measure (25 ft, marked in inches)
- Masking tape (1-inch wide, for

marking alignment points)
- Level (24-inch, for checking ground and wall)
- Floor jack (2-ton capacity) and jack stands (pair, rated for at least 2 tons each)
- Wheel chocks (set of 2, heavy-duty rubber)
- Shop light or headlamp (LED, 200+ lumens)
- Owner's manual (for bulb type, access, and alignment specs)

Step-by-step instructions

1. Park the vehicle on a level, paved surface facing a flat wall or garage door, at least 25 feet from the wall; engage the parking brake and place wheel chocks behind the rear tires
2. Check tire pressure and ensure all tires are inflated to the recommended PSI (see door jamb sticker); remove excess cargo from the vehicle and ensure the gas tank is at least half full for accurate alignment
3. Measure the distance from the ground to the center of each headlight lens using a tape measure; record the height
4. Use masking tape to mark two horizontal lines on the wall: one at the measured headlight height and another 2 inches below it; mark vertical lines corresponding to the center of each headlight (measure vehicle width and divide by two for center points)
5. Open the hood and secure with the prop rod; use a shop light to illuminate the headlight area
6. Disconnect the negative battery terminal using a 10mm socket to prevent electrical shorts
7. Locate the rear of the headlight assembly; remove any plastic covers or air intake ducts blocking access using a flathead screwdriver or 10mm socket as needed
8. Wearing nitrile gloves, disconnect the electrical connector from the back of the headlight bulb by pressing the release tab and pulling straight back
9. Rotate the bulb counterclockwise (typically 1/4 turn) and carefully remove it from the housing; avoid touching the glass with bare hands
10. Inspect the bulb socket and housing for corrosion or debris; clean with an alcohol wipe and allow to dry
11. Apply a thin layer of dielectric grease to the bulb's metal base or terminals to prevent corrosion
12. Insert the new bulb into the housing, aligning the tabs; rotate clockwise until it locks securely in place
13. Reconnect the electrical connector, ensuring a firm click; replace any covers or ducts removed earlier
14. Repeat the process for the opposite headlight if needed
15. Reconnect the negative battery terminal and tighten securely
16. Turn on the headlights and check for proper operation; ensure both low and high beams function
17. For beam alignment, position the vehicle exactly 25 feet from the wall; bounce the suspension by pressing down on each corner to settle the vehicle
18. Turn on low beams; observe the cutoff line on the wall. The top of the most intense part of the beam should be at or just below the lower tape line (2 inches below headlight center height)
19. Locate the vertical and

horizontal adjustment screws on the headlight assembly (refer to owner's manual for exact location; typically accessible from above or behind the housing)

20. Use a Phillips screwdriver to turn the vertical adjustment screw: clockwise to raise, counterclockwise to lower the beam. Adjust until the cutoff aligns with the lower tape line
21. Adjust the horizontal screw to center the beam pattern on the vertical tape mark for each headlight
22. Repeat adjustments for both headlights, ensuring beams are even and not aimed too high or outward
23. Test high beams to confirm they are also properly aligned; make minor adjustments if necessary
24. Remove masking tape from the wall and close the hood

Illustrations and diagrams

Diagram of headlight assembly with bulb access points and adjustment screw locations
Cross-section of headlight housing showing bulb installation and locking mechanism
Schematic of vehicle positioned 25 feet from wall with tape alignment marks
Step-by-step visual of bulb removal, installation, and beam alignment process

Practical expert tips

Always wear gloves when handling new bulbs; oils from your skin can cause hot spots and premature failure
Replace headlight bulbs in pairs to ensure even brightness and color temperature
Mark the date and mileage of bulb replacement in your maintenance log or on a sticker near the headlight housing
If the headlight lens is cloudy or yellowed, clean or restore it before aligning beams for best results
Use a level to confirm both the ground and wall are perfectly flat for accurate alignment

Troubleshooting techniques

If the new bulb does not light, check the electrical connector for corrosion or loose pins; test voltage at the connector with a multimeter (should read 12V with headlights on)
If the beam pattern is scattered or dim, inspect the headlight lens for internal condensation or damage; replace or reseal as needed
If the adjustment screws are seized, apply penetrating oil and gently work them back and forth; avoid forcing to prevent breakage
If one side remains dim after bulb replacement, check the vehicle's fuse box for a blown headlight fuse and replace with the correct amperage
If the beam is still misaligned after adjustment, verify the vehicle is unloaded and on level ground; recheck tire pressure and repeat alignment

Security and preventive maintenance

Inspect headlight operation and alignment every 6 months or before long road trips
Clean headlight lenses monthly with a plastic-safe cleaner to maintain maximum brightness
Check for moisture inside the

headlight housing after heavy rain or car washes; reseal or replace gaskets if needed
Always use bulbs with the correct wattage and type specified in your owner's manual to avoid electrical damage or overheating
Store spare bulbs in their original packaging in a cool, dry place away from direct sunlight

Taillight, Brake Light, and Turn Signal Socket Repair

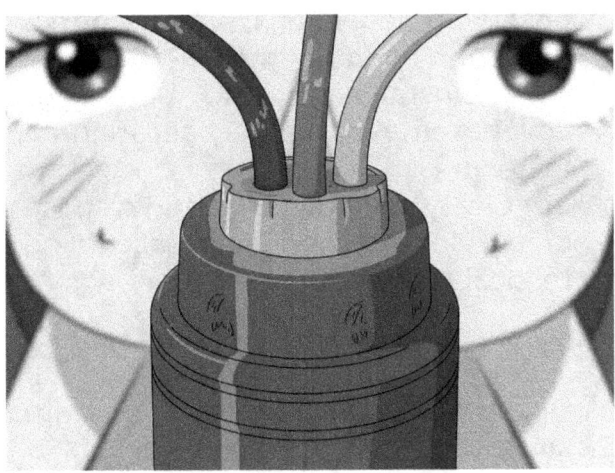

Materials and Tools

- Replacement bulb sockets (OEM or high-quality aftermarket, specify type: 1157 dual-filament, 3157, etc.; check owner's manual for correct fit)
- Replacement bulbs (match socket type and wattage, e.g., 1157 12V 27/8W for dual-filament)
- 16–18 gauge automotive primary wire (stranded copper, temperature rated to 221°F/105°C)
- Heat-shrink tubing (3/16-inch diameter, adhesive-lined, 4-inch lengths)
- Soldering iron (30–40W) and rosin-core solder (0.032-inch diameter)
- Wire strippers (10–20 AWG range)
- Crimp connectors (butt splice, heat-shrink type, 16–18 gauge)
- Crimping tool (ratcheting, for insulated connectors)
- Multimeter (digital, with continuity and voltage test functions)
- Dielectric grease (0.5 oz tube)
- Electrical contact cleaner (aerosol, 11 oz can)
- Small flathead screwdriver (1/8-inch tip)
- Phillips screwdriver (#2)
- 10mm socket and ratchet (for taillight assembly bolts)
- Trim removal tool (nylon, 6-inch)
- Utility knife (retractable, for wire insulation)
- Clean microfiber towels (16x16 inch, lint-free, set of 2)
- Nitrile gloves (5–7 mil thickness)
- Safety glasses (ANSI Z87.1 rated)
- Shop light or headlamp (LED, 200+ lumens)
- Owner's manual (for bulb and socket specifications)

Step-by-step instructions

1. Park the vehicle on a flat, paved surface; engage the parking brake and turn off the ignition
2. Open the trunk or tailgate to access the rear of the taillight assembly; use a shop light for clear visibility
3. Remove any interior trim panels or covers blocking access to the taillight using a trim removal tool; set aside all fasteners
4. Locate the taillight, brake light, or turn signal socket at the rear of the assembly; identify the faulty socket by testing each function (turn signal, brake, taillight) with a helper or by observing bulb operation
5. Disconnect the electrical connector from the socket by pressing the release tab and pulling

straight back
6. Rotate the socket counterclockwise (typically 1/4 turn) and remove it from the taillight housing
7. Remove the bulb from the socket by pressing in and turning counterclockwise (bayonet base) or pulling straight out (wedge base)
8. Inspect the socket for corrosion, melted plastic, or loose terminals; clean minor corrosion with electrical contact cleaner and a small screwdriver, wiping dry with a microfiber towel
9. If the socket is damaged or corroded beyond cleaning, cut the wires 2 inches behind the socket using a utility knife and wire strippers; strip 1/2 inch of insulation from each wire end
10. Prepare the replacement socket by stripping 1/2 inch of insulation from each wire; slide a 4-inch length of heat-shrink tubing over each vehicle wire before making connections
11. Match wire colors from the vehicle harness to the new socket (typically black for ground, colored for signal/brake/taillight); if unsure, use a multimeter to confirm function by probing each wire with the light switch or brake pedal activated
12. For soldered connections: twist matching wires together, heat with a soldering iron, and apply rosin-core solder until the joint is fully wetted; slide heat-shrink tubing over the joint and shrink with a heat gun or lighter until fully sealed
13. For crimped connections: insert stripped wire ends into a butt splice connector, crimp firmly with a ratcheting tool, and heat the connector to shrink and seal
14. Apply a small amount of dielectric grease to the socket terminals to prevent future corrosion
15. Insert the replacement bulb into the new socket, ensuring correct orientation and firm seating
16. Reinstall the socket into the taillight housing, rotating clockwise until it locks securely
17. Reconnect the electrical connector to the socket; ensure a positive click
18. Test all functions (taillight, brake light, turn signal) with a helper or by observing reflections; verify correct operation and brightness
19. Reinstall any trim panels or covers removed earlier, securing all fasteners
20. Clean the work area and dispose of old sockets and bulbs according to local regulations

Illustrations and diagrams

Diagram of taillight assembly with socket and bulb locations labeled
Cross-section of bulb socket showing terminal and wire connections
Schematic of wire color codes for taillight, brake, and turn signal circuits
Step-by-step visual of socket removal, wire splicing, and reinstallation process

Practical expert tips

Always replace bulbs in pairs (left and right) to ensure even brightness and color temperature
Mark the date and mileage of socket repair in your maintenance log or on a sticker inside the trunk
Use adhesive-lined heat-shrink tubing for maximum moisture protection on all wire splices

If the socket is difficult to access, remove the entire taillight assembly using a 10mm socket and ratchet for easier handling
For vehicles with LED taillights, check for integrated circuit boards; socket repair may require a full assembly replacement

Troubleshooting techniques

If the new bulb does not light, check for 12V at the socket terminals with a multimeter while the function is activated
If only one function (e.g., brake or turn) fails, verify correct wire connections and check for blown fuses in the vehicle's fuse box
If bulbs burn out quickly, inspect for poor ground connections or excessive voltage (should not exceed 14.5V with engine running)
If the socket is loose in the housing, gently bend the metal tabs outward with a small screwdriver for a tighter fit
If corrosion returns quickly, check for water leaks in the taillight housing and reseal with automotive-grade silicone

Security and preventive maintenance

Inspect taillight, brake, and turn signal operation monthly, especially before long trips or state inspections
Clean sockets and apply dielectric grease at every bulb change to prevent corrosion
Check for water intrusion in taillight housings after heavy rain or car washes; repair seals as needed
Always wear gloves and safety glasses to protect against sharp edges and electrical contact

Store spare bulbs and sockets in a cool, dry place away from direct sunlight and moisture

Interior Dome and Courtesy Light Switch Replacement

Materials and Tools

- Replacement dome/courtesy light switch (OEM or high-quality aftermarket, specify type: push-button, rocker, or plunger; check owner's manual for correct fit)
- Replacement bulbs (festoon 31mm 12V 10W, or wedge T10 12V 5W, as specified for your vehicle)
- 1/4-inch drive ratchet and socket set (7mm, 8mm, 10mm sockets)
- Phillips screwdriver (#2)
- Flathead screwdriver (1/4-inch tip, for prying)
- Trim removal tool (nylon, 6-inch)
- Multimeter (digital, with continuity and voltage test functions)
- Needle-nose pliers (6-inch, insulated handles)
- Dielectric grease (0.5 oz tube)
- Electrical contact cleaner (aerosol, 11 oz can)
- Clean microfiber towels (16x16 inch, lint-free, set of 2)
- Nitrile gloves (5–7 mil thickness)
- Safety glasses (ANSI Z87.1 rated)

- Shop light or headlamp (LED, 200+ lumens)
- Owner's manual (for switch and bulb specifications)

Step-by-step instructions

1. Park the vehicle on a flat, paved surface; engage the parking brake and turn off the ignition
2. Disconnect the negative battery terminal using a 10mm socket to prevent accidental short circuits
3. Put on nitrile gloves and safety glasses for protection against sharp trim edges and electrical contact
4. Use a shop light or headlamp to illuminate the dome/courtesy light area for clear visibility
5. For dome/courtesy lights mounted in the headliner: insert a nylon trim removal tool between the light housing and headliner, gently prying around the perimeter to release retaining clips; avoid using metal tools to prevent damage
6. For door jamb switches: open the door fully, locate the switch (typically a plunger-style unit near the hinge), and use a Phillips screwdriver or appropriate socket to remove the mounting screw(s)
7. Carefully pull the light housing or switch out, exposing the wiring harness; do not force, as wires may be short
8. Disconnect the electrical connector by pressing the release tab and pulling straight back; if wires are attached with spade terminals, use needle-nose pliers to gently remove them
9. Inspect the connector and terminals for corrosion or debris; clean with electrical contact cleaner and a microfiber towel, allowing to dry completely
10. Use a multimeter to check for 12V at the connector with the door open or switch activated; verify ground continuity to ensure proper circuit function
11. If replacing a bulb, remove the old bulb (twist or pull out, depending on type) and install the new one, ensuring correct orientation and firm seating
12. Apply a small amount of dielectric grease to the switch terminals to prevent future corrosion
13. Connect the wiring harness to the new switch or light assembly, ensuring a positive click or secure fit
14. For door jamb switches: align the new switch in the mounting hole, secure with the original screw(s), and tighten snugly (do not overtighten to avoid cracking plastic)
15. For dome/courtesy lights: position the housing in the headliner opening, press evenly until all retaining clips snap into place
16. Reconnect the negative battery terminal and tighten securely
17. Test the dome/courtesy light and switch operation by opening and closing the door, and by manually activating the switch if applicable; verify proper illumination and switch function
18. Clean the work area and dispose of old switches and bulbs according to local regulations

Illustrations and diagrams

Diagram of dome/courtesy light assembly with bulb and switch locations labeled
Cross-section of door jamb switch showing plunger mechanism and wiring
Schematic of wiring harness

connector and typical color codes for dome/courtesy light circuits
Step-by-step visual of trim removal, switch disconnection, and reinstallation process

Practical expert tips

Always replace bulbs and switches in pairs (driver and passenger side) to ensure even operation and brightness
Mark the date and mileage of switch or bulb replacement in your maintenance log or on a sticker inside the fuse box cover
Use a nylon trim tool to avoid marring headliner or plastic trim when removing light housings
If the switch is difficult to access, remove adjacent trim panels for better reach and visibility
For intermittent dome light issues, check for loose ground wires or worn door hinges that may affect switch alignment

Troubleshooting techniques

If the new switch does not activate the light, check for 12V at the connector with the door open; if absent, inspect the fuse (typically 10A, labeled "DOME" or "INTERIOR") and replace if blown
If the light stays on with the door closed, verify that the switch plunger is fully depressed when the door is shut; adjust or shim the switch if necessary
If the bulb flickers, inspect for loose socket connections or corroded terminals; clean and apply dielectric grease as needed
If multiple interior lights fail, check for a shared ground point or body control module issue; consult the wiring diagram in the owner's manual

Security and preventive maintenance

Inspect dome and courtesy light operation monthly, especially before long trips or nighttime driving
Clean switch and bulb contacts with electrical contact cleaner at every bulb change to prevent corrosion
Check for water leaks around door seals that may cause switch corrosion; repair seals as needed
Always use bulbs and switches with the correct specifications listed in your owner's manual to avoid electrical issues
Store spare bulbs and switches in a cool, dry place away from direct sunlight and moisture

Fuse Box Diagnosis and Corroded Connector Repair

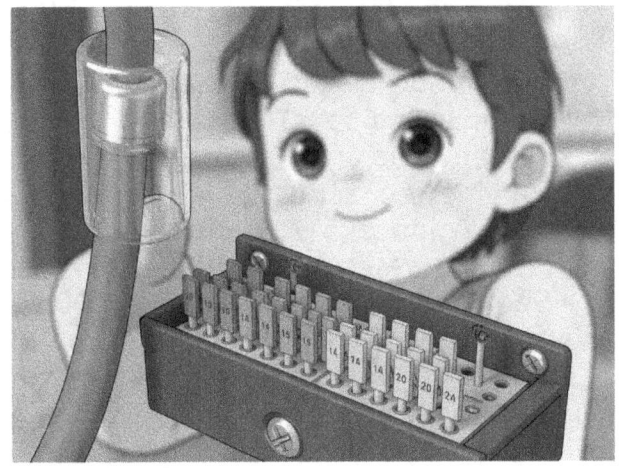

Materials and Tools

- Replacement fuses (ATO/ATC blade type, mini or micro, 5A–30A as specified in owner's manual)
- OEM or high-quality aftermarket fuse puller (plastic, non-conductive,

3-inch)
- Digital multimeter (auto-ranging, 10A/600V, with continuity and voltage test functions)
- Electrical contact cleaner (aerosol, 11 oz can)
- Dielectric grease (0.5 oz tube)
- Small brass wire brush (1/4-inch width, non-sparking)
- Nylon bristle brush (6-inch, for delicate cleaning)
- 16–18 gauge automotive primary wire (stranded copper, temperature rated to 221°F/105°C)
- Heat-shrink tubing (3/16-inch diameter, adhesive-lined, 4-inch lengths)
- Soldering iron (30–40W) and rosin-core solder (0.032-inch diameter)
- Wire strippers (10–20 AWG range)
- Crimp connectors (butt splice, heat-shrink type, 16–18 gauge)
- Crimping tool (ratcheting, for insulated connectors)
- Needle-nose pliers (6-inch, insulated handles)
- Flathead screwdriver (1/4-inch tip)
- Phillips screwdriver (#2)
- 10mm socket and ratchet (for fuse box mounting bolts)
- Clean microfiber towels (16x16 inch, lint-free, set of 2)
- Nitrile gloves (5–7 mil thickness)
- Safety glasses (ANSI Z87.1 rated)
- Shop light or headlamp (LED, 200+ lumens)
- Owner's manual (for fuse box diagram and specifications)

Step-by-step instructions

1. Park the vehicle on a flat, paved surface; engage the parking brake and turn off the ignition
2. Disconnect the negative battery terminal using a 10mm socket to prevent accidental short circuits
3. Put on nitrile gloves and safety glasses for protection against electrical contact and sharp edges
4. Use a shop light or headlamp to illuminate the fuse box area for clear visibility
5. Locate the main fuse box (under the hood or beneath the dashboard, as specified in the owner's manual); remove the cover by releasing retaining clips or screws with a flathead or Phillips screwdriver
6. Refer to the fuse box diagram (on the cover or in the manual) to identify the circuit(s) experiencing issues (e.g., headlights, radio, power windows)
7. Use a fuse puller to remove the suspect fuse; inspect the metal strip for breaks or discoloration indicating a blown fuse
8. Test the suspect fuse with a multimeter set to continuity mode; place probes on each blade—no beep or reading means the fuse is blown
9. Replace blown fuses with new ones of identical amperage rating (e.g., 15A for a 15A circuit); never substitute a higher-rated fuse
10. If the new fuse blows immediately, suspect a short circuit or corroded connector; proceed to inspect the fuse box terminals and wiring
11. Visually inspect all fuse box terminals and connectors for signs of corrosion (green/white powder, discoloration, or pitting)
12. For minor corrosion, spray electrical contact cleaner directly onto the affected terminal; scrub gently with a brass wire brush or nylon bristle brush until clean
13. Wipe the area dry with a clean microfiber towel; repeat cleaning if

necessary until all corrosion is removed

14. For severe corrosion or damaged terminals, use needle-nose pliers to carefully remove the affected connector from the fuse box (release locking tabs if present)
15. Cut the corroded wire 2 inches behind the terminal using wire strippers; strip 1/2 inch of insulation from the wire end
16. Prepare a new length of 16–18 gauge automotive wire if needed; strip 1/2 inch of insulation from both ends
17. Slide a 4-inch length of heat-shrink tubing over the wire before making connections
18. For soldered repair: twist the new wire to the existing wire, heat with a soldering iron, and apply rosin-core solder until the joint is fully wetted; slide heat-shrink tubing over the joint and shrink with a heat gun or lighter until fully sealed
19. For crimped repair: insert stripped wire ends into a butt splice connector, crimp firmly with a ratcheting tool, and heat the connector to shrink and seal
20. Attach a new terminal to the repaired wire (crimp or solder as required); insert the terminal back into the fuse box until it clicks securely
21. Apply a small amount of dielectric grease to all cleaned or repaired terminals to prevent future corrosion
22. Reinstall the fuse box cover, ensuring all clips or screws are secure
23. Reconnect the negative battery terminal and tighten securely
24. Test all affected circuits by operating the relevant switches (e.g., headlights, radio, power windows) to confirm proper function
25. Clean the work area and dispose of old fuses, corroded wire, and cleaning materials according to local regulations

Illustrations and diagrams

Diagram of fuse box layout with fuse and connector locations labeled
Cross-section of a corroded fuse box terminal before and after cleaning
Schematic of wire splicing and terminal replacement process
Step-by-step visual of fuse removal, corrosion cleaning, and connector repair

Practical expert tips

Always use fuses with the exact amperage specified in your owner's manual to avoid electrical fires or component damage
Mark the date and mileage of fuse or connector repair in your maintenance log or on a sticker inside the fuse box cover
Use adhesive-lined heat-shrink tubing for maximum moisture protection on all wire splices and repairs
If the fuse box is difficult to access, remove adjacent trim panels or mounting bolts for better reach and visibility
For recurring corrosion, check for water leaks in the engine bay or cabin and reseal with automotive-grade silicone

Troubleshooting techniques

If a new fuse blows instantly, use a multimeter to check for continuity to ground on the load side of the fuse terminal; a reading near zero ohms

indicates a short circuit downstream

If multiple circuits fail, inspect the main power feed and ground connections to the fuse box for corrosion or looseness

If a circuit is intermittent, gently wiggle the fuse and connector while monitoring voltage with a multimeter to detect loose or oxidized contacts

If cleaning does not restore function, check for melted plastic or heat damage in the fuse box; replacement of the entire fuse box may be necessary

Security and preventive maintenance

Inspect fuse box and connector condition every 6 months, especially after heavy rain, snow, or engine bay cleaning

Clean and apply dielectric grease to fuse terminals at every major service interval (12,000–15,000 miles)

Check for water intrusion around fuse box seals and grommets; repair or replace as needed to prevent future corrosion

Always disconnect the battery before working on the fuse box to avoid accidental shorts or electrical shock

Store spare fuses, terminals, and cleaning supplies in a cool, dry place away from direct sunlight and moisture

4: LIGHTING AND ELECTRICAL REPAIR PROJECTS

Daytime Running Light Troubleshooting and Module Replacement

Materials and Tools

- Replacement daytime running light (DRL) module (OEM or high-quality aftermarket, matched to vehicle year/make/model)
- Replacement DRL bulbs (9005 12V 60W halogen, or LED equivalent as specified in owner's manual)
- Digital multimeter (auto-ranging, 10A/600V, with continuity and voltage test functions)
- 1/4-inch drive ratchet and socket set (8mm, 10mm, 12mm sockets)
- Torx bit set (T20, T25, T30)
- Phillips screwdriver (#2)
- Flathead screwdriver (1/4-inch tip)
- Trim removal tool (nylon, 6-inch)
- Needle-nose pliers (6-inch, insulated handles)
- Dielectric grease (0.5 oz tube)
- Electrical contact cleaner (aerosol, 11 oz can)
- Heat-shrink tubing (3/16-inch diameter, adhesive-lined, 4-inch lengths)
- Wire strippers (10–20 AWG range)
- Crimp connectors (butt splice, heat-shrink type, 16–18 gauge)

- Crimping tool (ratcheting, for insulated connectors)
- Shop light or headlamp (LED, 200+ lumens)
- Clean microfiber towels (16x16 inch, lint-free, set of 2)
- Nitrile gloves (5–7 mil thickness)
- Safety glasses (ANSI Z87.1 rated)
- Owner's manual (for DRL circuit diagram and specifications)

Step-by-step instructions

1. Park the vehicle on a flat, paved surface; engage the parking brake and turn off the ignition
2. Disconnect the negative battery terminal using a 10mm socket to prevent accidental short circuits
3. Put on nitrile gloves and safety glasses for protection against electrical contact and sharp edges
4. Use a shop light or headlamp to illuminate the DRL module and light housing area for clear visibility
5. Locate the DRL module (commonly under the hood near the radiator support, inside the fuse/relay box, or behind the front bumper; refer to owner's manual for exact location)
6. Remove any covers or trim panels blocking access to the DRL module using a nylon trim tool, Phillips screwdriver, or Torx bits as required
7. Visually inspect the DRL bulbs for discoloration, broken filaments, or cloudiness; replace with new bulbs if defective
8. Use a multimeter to check for 12V at the DRL bulb socket with the ignition on and parking brake released; if no voltage is present, proceed to test the DRL module
9. Disconnect the electrical connector from the DRL module by pressing the release tab and pulling straight back; inspect for corrosion or bent pins
10. Clean the connector and module pins with electrical contact cleaner and a microfiber towel; allow to dry completely
11. Set the multimeter to continuity mode; check for continuity between the DRL module ground pin and chassis ground (should read less than 1 ohm)
12. With the ignition on and parking brake released, set the multimeter to DC voltage; probe the DRL module input pin for 12V supply voltage
13. If supply voltage and ground are present but DRLs do not operate, the module is likely faulty and requires replacement
14. Remove the DRL module mounting bolts using the appropriate socket or Torx bit; retain hardware for reinstallation
15. If wiring repair is needed, cut damaged wire 2 inches behind the connector using wire strippers; strip 1/2 inch of insulation from both ends
16. Slide a 4-inch length of heat-shrink tubing over the wire before making connections
17. For crimped repair: insert stripped wire ends into a butt splice connector, crimp firmly with a ratcheting tool, and heat the connector to shrink and seal
18. For soldered repair: twist the new wire to the existing wire, heat with a soldering iron, and apply rosin-core solder until the joint is fully wetted; slide heat-shrink tubing over the joint and shrink with a heat gun or lighter until fully sealed
19. Install the new DRL module in the original location; secure with mounting bolts and tighten snugly

(do not overtighten to avoid cracking plastic)
20. Apply a small amount of dielectric grease to the module connector pins to prevent future corrosion
21. Reconnect the electrical connector to the new DRL module, ensuring a positive click or secure fit
22. Reinstall any covers or trim panels removed earlier, ensuring all clips or screws are secure
23. Reconnect the negative battery terminal and tighten securely
24. Test DRL operation by starting the vehicle, releasing the parking brake, and verifying that the DRLs illuminate as intended
25. Clean the work area and dispose of old modules, bulbs, and cleaning materials according to local regulations

Illustrations and diagrams

Diagram of DRL module location and mounting points in a typical engine bay
Cross-section of DRL bulb socket and wiring harness with voltage test points labeled
Schematic of DRL circuit showing module, bulbs, and input/output connections
Step-by-step visual of module removal, connector cleaning, and reinstallation process

Practical expert tips

Always replace DRL bulbs in pairs to ensure even brightness and color temperature
Mark the date and mileage of DRL module or bulb replacement in your maintenance log or on a sticker inside the fuse box cover
Use a nylon trim tool to avoid marring plastic trim or painted surfaces when removing covers
If the DRL module is difficult to access, remove adjacent components (air intake duct, battery, or headlight assembly) for better reach and visibility
For vehicles with LED DRLs, check for polarity before installing new bulbs or modules; LEDs will not function if installed backward

Troubleshooting techniques

If new DRL bulbs do not illuminate, verify 12V supply at the socket with the ignition on and parking brake released; if absent, check the DRL fuse (typically 10A–15A, labeled "DRL" or "DAYTIME") and replace if blown
If the DRLs flicker or operate intermittently, inspect for loose or corroded connectors at the module and bulb sockets; clean and apply dielectric grease as needed
If only one DRL is out, swap bulbs side-to-side to confirm if the issue is with the bulb or the wiring/module
If the DRLs stay on with the ignition off, suspect a stuck relay or faulty module; replace as necessary
For vehicles with DRL integrated into the headlight assembly, check for melted or discolored bulb sockets indicating excessive heat or poor contact

Security and preventive maintenance

Inspect DRL operation monthly, especially before long trips or during seasonal changes when daylight hours vary
Clean DRL lenses and bulb contacts

with electrical contact cleaner at every bulb change to maintain optimal brightness
Check for water intrusion around DRL housings and module connectors; repair seals or gaskets as needed to prevent corrosion
Always use bulbs and modules with the correct specifications listed in your owner's manual to avoid electrical issues
Store spare DRL bulbs and modules in a cool, dry place away from direct sunlight and moisture

LED Headlight Retrofit and Beam Pattern Adjustment

Materials and Tools

- LED headlight retrofit kit (9005, H11, H4, or as specified in owner's manual; 6000K color temperature, 4000–6000 lumens per bulb, CANbus compatible if required)
- Anti-flicker harness or decoder (if vehicle has bulb-out warning or flicker issues)
- Headlight beam pattern alignment tool (bubble level or laser alignment tool, 24-inch)
- 1/4-inch drive ratchet and socket set (8mm, 10mm, 12mm sockets)
- Phillips screwdriver (#2)
- Flathead screwdriver (1/4-inch tip)
- Torx bit set (T20, T25)
- Trim removal tool (nylon, 6-inch)
- Dielectric grease (0.5 oz tube)
- Electrical contact cleaner (aerosol, 11 oz can)
- Clean microfiber towels (16x16 inch, lint-free, set of 2)
- Nitrile gloves (5–7 mil thickness)
- Safety glasses (ANSI Z87.1 rated)
- Measuring tape (25-foot, marked in 1/8-inch increments)
- Masking tape (1-inch wide, 30-yard roll)
- Shop light or headlamp (LED, 200+ lumens)
- Owner's manual (for bulb type, headlight housing access, and aiming specifications)

Step-by-step instructions

1. Park the vehicle on a level, paved surface facing a flat wall or garage door, with at least 25 feet of clear space in front; ensure the fuel tank is half full and tire pressures are set to manufacturer specs
2. Measure the distance from the ground to the center of each headlight lens using a measuring tape; record this height
3. Mark the headlight center height on the wall with horizontal strips of masking tape, one for each headlight, at the same height as measured from the ground
4. Place vertical strips of masking tape on the wall to mark the centerline of each headlight, aligning with the vehicle's center and each headlight's center point
5. Turn off the ignition and headlights; disconnect the negative battery terminal using a 10mm socket to prevent electrical shorts

THE CAR MAINTENANCE AND REPAIR BIBLE

6. Put on nitrile gloves and safety glasses to protect against sharp edges and electrical contact
7. Open the hood and locate the rear of the headlight assemblies; remove any covers, air intake ducts, or battery if necessary for access using a trim tool, ratchet, or screwdriver
8. Disconnect the headlight bulb connector by pressing the release tab and pulling straight back; inspect for corrosion or bent pins
9. Clean the connector with electrical contact cleaner and a microfiber towel; allow to dry completely
10. Remove the halogen bulb by rotating counterclockwise (typically 1/4 turn); avoid touching the glass of halogen bulbs with bare hands
11. Insert the LED bulb into the headlight housing, aligning the tabs for a secure fit; rotate clockwise until locked in place
12. Connect the LED bulb's wiring harness to the vehicle's headlight connector; if required, install the anti-flicker harness or decoder between the bulb and connector
13. Apply a small amount of dielectric grease to the connector pins to prevent future corrosion
14. Secure any external LED drivers or ballasts using zip ties or adhesive pads, keeping them away from moving parts and heat sources
15. Reinstall any covers, ducts, or components removed for access; ensure all clips and screws are secure
16. Reconnect the negative battery terminal and tighten securely
17. Turn on the headlights and check for proper LED operation; verify both low and high beams function as intended
18. With the headlights on low beam, observe the beam pattern on the wall at 25 feet; the top of the brightest part of the beam should be at or just below the horizontal tape line, and the beam cutoff should be sharp and level
19. If adjustment is needed, locate the vertical and horizontal adjustment screws on the headlight assembly (refer to owner's manual for location and direction)
20. Use a Phillips screwdriver or Torx bit to turn the adjustment screws: clockwise to raise or move the beam right, counterclockwise to lower or move left; adjust until the beam cutoff aligns with the tape marks and does not exceed the horizontal line
21. Repeat the process for the other headlight, ensuring both beams are level and symmetrical
22. Test high beams to confirm proper function and that the pattern does not blind oncoming drivers
23. Clean the work area and dispose of old bulbs and packaging according to local regulations

Illustrations and diagrams

Diagram of headlight assembly with bulb, connector, and adjustment screw locations labeled
Step-by-step visual of LED bulb installation and harness connection
Wall aiming chart showing correct tape placement and beam cutoff alignment at 25 feet
Schematic of anti-flicker harness installation between LED bulb and vehicle connector

Practical expert tips

Always choose LED bulbs with a

focused beam pattern and correct filament position to mimic halogen output and avoid glare

Mark the date and mileage of LED retrofit in your maintenance log or on a sticker inside the engine bay

If the headlight housing has a dust cover, ensure it is fully sealed after installation to prevent moisture intrusion

For vehicles with projector headlights, select LED bulbs specifically designed for projector use to maintain proper cutoff and focus

If the LED bulb's heat sink or fan is large, check for clearance before installation to avoid interference with other components

Troubleshooting techniques

If the LED headlights flicker or trigger a bulb-out warning, install a CANbus-compatible anti-flicker harness or decoder

If one or both LEDs do not illuminate, check polarity by reversing the connector; LEDs are polarity-sensitive

If the beam pattern is scattered or causes glare, verify the bulb is fully seated and oriented correctly; adjust or reinstall as needed

If condensation appears inside the headlight housing after installation, check that all seals and covers are properly reinstalled and undamaged

If the high beam indicator stays on with low beams, use an LED kit with built-in resistors or consult the manufacturer for a compatible solution

Security and preventive maintenance

Inspect headlight operation and beam alignment every 6 months or after any front-end collision or suspension work

Clean headlight lenses with a non-abrasive plastic polish at every oil change to maintain maximum light output

Check for loose connectors, damaged wiring, or moisture inside the housing during routine maintenance

Store spare halogen bulbs in the glove box as a backup in case of LED failure during travel

Always use LED bulbs and components that meet DOT or SAE standards for on-road use to ensure safety and legality

Alternator Output Test and Voltage Regulator Replacement for Charging Repairs

Materials and Tools

- Digital multimeter (auto-ranging, minimum 10A/600V, with min/max voltage capture)
- 3/8-inch drive ratchet and socket set (10mm, 12mm, 13mm, 15mm sockets)

- Combination wrenches (10mm, 12mm, 13mm)
- Insulated screwdriver set (Phillips #2, flathead 1/4-inch tip)
- Replacement voltage regulator (OEM or high-quality aftermarket, matched to alternator model and vehicle year/make/model)
- Replacement alternator (if regulator is internal and alternator is non-serviceable)
- Battery terminal puller (if terminals are corroded or seized)
- Battery post and terminal cleaner (wire brush, 4-in-1 tool)
- Nitrile gloves (5–7 mil thickness)
- Safety glasses (ANSI Z87.1 rated)
- Shop light or headlamp (LED, 200+ lumens)
- Clean microfiber towels (16x16 inch, lint-free, set of 2)
- Dielectric grease (0.5 oz tube)
- Torque wrench (5–80 ft-lb range)
- Owner's manual (for alternator location, belt routing, and torque specs)
- Service manual or alternator wiring diagram (for voltage regulator pinout and test points)

Step-by-step instructions

1. Park the vehicle on a flat, paved surface; engage the parking brake and turn off the ignition
2. Open the hood and locate the alternator (typically mounted at the front of the engine, driven by the serpentine or V-belt)
3. Put on nitrile gloves and safety glasses for protection against battery acid and moving parts
4. Set the digital multimeter to DC voltage (20V range); connect the red probe to the battery positive terminal and the black probe to the negative terminal
5. Record the battery voltage with the engine off; a healthy battery should read 12.4–12.7V
6. Start the engine and let it idle; observe the multimeter reading at the battery terminals
7. A properly functioning alternator should produce 13.8–14.6V at idle; if voltage is below 13.5V or above 14.8V, proceed with further testing
8. Turn on headlights, blower fan, and rear defroster to apply electrical load; observe voltage drop—voltage should remain above 13.2V
9. If voltage is low or fluctuates, turn off the engine and disconnect the negative battery terminal using a 10mm wrench
10. Inspect alternator belt tension and condition; press down at the midpoint—deflection should be 1/4–1/2 inch; replace or tighten as needed
11. Locate the voltage regulator (external: mounted on fender/firewall; internal: inside alternator housing)
12. For external regulator: disconnect wiring harness and mounting bolts using appropriate sockets; remove regulator
13. For internal regulator: remove serpentine or V-belt by rotating the tensioner with a 3/8-inch ratchet; note belt routing with a diagram or photo
14. Disconnect alternator electrical connectors (main output terminal, field wire, and ground) using a 10mm or 12mm wrench; label wires if needed
15. Remove alternator mounting bolts (typically 13mm or 15mm); support alternator and lift out of engine bay
16. Place alternator on a clean

workbench; remove rear cover screws (Phillips or 8mm socket) to access internal regulator

17. Unscrew and remove the voltage regulator; compare new regulator to old for correct fit and pin configuration
18. Install new voltage regulator, ensuring all screws are tight and electrical contacts are clean; apply a thin layer of dielectric grease to connector pins
19. Reassemble alternator and reinstall in vehicle; torque mounting bolts to manufacturer specs (typically 25–35 ft-lb)
20. Reconnect all electrical connectors and main output terminal; ensure all connections are tight and free of corrosion
21. Reinstall serpentine or V-belt, following the correct routing; use a torque wrench to set tensioner bolt if required
22. Reconnect the negative battery terminal and tighten securely
23. Start the engine and repeat the voltage test at the battery terminals; confirm charging voltage is within 13.8–14.6V at idle and under load
24. Clean the work area and dispose of old regulator or alternator according to local regulations

Illustrations and diagrams

Diagram of alternator location and mounting points in a typical engine bay

Schematic of alternator wiring and voltage regulator pinout (external and internal types)

Step-by-step visual of alternator removal, regulator replacement, and reinstallation

Multimeter connection points for battery and alternator output testing

Practical expert tips

Always test battery health before diagnosing alternator issues; a weak battery can mimic charging problems

Mark the date and mileage of voltage regulator or alternator replacement in your maintenance log or on a sticker inside the engine bay

Use a shop light to inspect for frayed wires or loose connectors at the alternator and regulator

If the alternator is difficult to access, remove adjacent components (air intake duct, radiator fan shroud) for better reach

For vehicles with smart charging systems, consult the service manual for special test procedures or scan tool requirements

Troubleshooting techniques

If charging voltage is still low after regulator replacement, check for blown alternator fuse (typically 80A–150A, located in the main fuse box) and replace if necessary

If voltage is too high (over 15V), suspect a faulty new regulator or poor ground connection; clean and retighten all grounds

If the battery warning light stays on, verify continuity of the field wire from the alternator to the dashboard indicator

If alternator whines or makes grinding noises after reinstallation, check for misaligned or overtightened belt and correct as needed

If voltage fluctuates with engine RPM, inspect for loose or corroded battery terminals and alternator output connections

Security and preventive maintenance

Inspect alternator output and battery voltage every 6 months or before long trips
Clean battery terminals and alternator connectors with a wire brush and apply dielectric grease at every service
Check alternator belt tension and condition at every oil change; replace if cracked, glazed, or frayed
Store spare fuses and a multimeter in your glove box for quick roadside diagnostics
Always use voltage regulators and alternators that meet OEM specifications to ensure safe and reliable charging system operation

Chassis Ground and Wiring Harness Corrosion Repair for Lighting Circuits

Materials and Tools

- Digital multimeter (auto-ranging, minimum 10A/600V, with continuity and resistance modes)
- 3/8-inch drive ratchet and socket set (8mm, 10mm, 12mm sockets)
- Combination wrenches (8mm, 10mm, 12mm)
- Wire brush (stainless steel, 6-inch handle)
- Small brass brush (for tight spaces, 4-inch)
- Dielectric grease (0.5 oz tube)
- Electrical contact cleaner (aerosol, 11 oz can)
- Heat shrink tubing (3/16-inch and 1/4-inch diameter, adhesive-lined, 6-inch lengths)
- Soldering iron (30–60W) and rosin-core solder (0.032-inch diameter)
- Crimping tool (ratcheting, for 22–10 AWG terminals)
- Heat gun (1200W, variable temperature)
- Replacement wire (automotive-grade, 16 AWG and 18 AWG, stranded copper, 10-foot lengths)
- Butt connectors (heat shrink, 16–18 AWG, blue and red, UL listed)
- Ring terminals (8mm and 10mm stud size, 16–18 AWG, tinned copper)
- Utility knife (retractable, with fresh blade)
- Wire strippers (10–20 AWG range)
- Nitrile gloves (5–7 mil thickness)
- Safety glasses (ANSI Z87.1 rated)
- Shop light or headlamp (LED, 200+ lumens)
- Clean microfiber towels (16x16 inch, lint-free, set of 2)
- Multimeter probe extension leads (24-inch, silicone insulated)
- Owner's manual and wiring diagram (for lighting circuit and ground locations)

Step-by-step instructions

1. Park the vehicle on a flat, paved surface; engage the parking brake and turn off the ignition
2. Open the hood and disconnect the negative battery terminal using a

10mm wrench to prevent accidental shorts

3. Locate the main chassis ground points for the lighting circuits using the wiring diagram; common locations include the radiator support, fender wells, and near headlight or taillight assemblies

4. Inspect ground points visually for corrosion, rust, or loose connections; use a shop light for clear visibility

5. Remove the ground bolt or screw using the appropriate socket or wrench; carefully detach the ring terminal from the chassis

6. Clean the chassis contact area with a wire brush until bare, shiny metal is exposed (minimum 1-inch diameter around the bolt hole)

7. Clean the ring terminal with a brass brush and electrical contact cleaner; dry thoroughly with a microfiber towel

8. If the ring terminal is heavily corroded or damaged, cut off the old terminal using a utility knife and wire strippers; strip 1/2 inch of insulation from the wire end

9. Crimp a new tinned copper ring terminal onto the stripped wire using a ratcheting crimp tool; for extra protection, use a heat shrink ring terminal and shrink with a heat gun until adhesive flows

10. Apply a thin layer of dielectric grease to both the chassis contact area and the ring terminal to prevent future corrosion

11. Reattach the ring terminal to the chassis using the original bolt; torque to manufacturer specs (typically 8–12 ft-lb)

12. For wiring harness repairs, trace the affected lighting circuit using the wiring diagram; look for greenish or white powder, cracked insulation, or stiff/brittle wires

13. Use a digital multimeter in continuity mode to check for open circuits between the lighting connector and the ground point; probe both ends with extension leads

14. If resistance exceeds 0.5 ohms or continuity fails, locate the corroded section by gently flexing the harness and probing at intervals

15. Cut out the damaged wire section using a utility knife; strip 1/2 inch of insulation from both ends of the good wire

16. Slide a 3-inch length of adhesive-lined heat shrink tubing over one wire end before joining

17. For a soldered repair: twist wire ends together, heat with a soldering iron, and flow rosin-core solder until fully wetted; allow to cool

18. For a crimped repair: insert both wire ends into a heat shrink butt connector and crimp securely with a ratcheting tool

19. Center the heat shrink tubing or use the built-in heat shrink on the connector; shrink with a heat gun until adhesive seals the joint

20. Secure the repaired section to the harness with zip ties, avoiding sharp bends or pinch points

21. Reconnect the negative battery terminal and tighten securely

22. Test the lighting circuit by turning on the headlights, parking lights, and turn signals; verify proper operation and brightness

23. Use a multimeter to confirm voltage at the lighting connector matches battery voltage (within 0.2V) with lights on

24. Clean the work area and dispose of old wire, terminals, and packaging according to local regulations

Illustrations and diagrams

Diagram of typical chassis ground locations in the engine bay and rear quarter panel
Step-by-step visual of ground point cleaning, terminal replacement, and reinstallation
Wiring harness cross-section showing corrosion, proper stripping, and heat shrink repair
Schematic of lighting circuit with ground path and test points labeled

Practical expert tips

Always disconnect the battery before working on ground points to avoid accidental short circuits
Mark the date and mileage of ground or harness repair in your maintenance log or on a sticker near the ground point
Use adhesive-lined heat shrink tubing for all repairs in exposed areas to prevent moisture intrusion
If a ground bolt is rusted or stripped, replace with a new zinc-plated or stainless steel bolt of the same thread and length
For persistent ground issues, add a supplemental ground strap (10 AWG braided copper, 12-inch) between the chassis and engine block

Troubleshooting techniques

If lighting remains dim or intermittent after repair, check for additional ground points or harness splices further along the circuit
If a new ground repair does not resolve the issue, test for voltage drop between the battery negative and the lighting ground with the circuit active; a drop over 0.2V indicates a poor connection
If corrosion recurs rapidly, inspect for coolant or washer fluid leaks above the harness or ground point and repair as needed
If multiple circuits are affected, check the main body ground strap from the battery to the chassis for looseness or corrosion

Security and preventive maintenance

Inspect all lighting ground points and harnesses every 12 months or after driving in salted or wet conditions
Apply dielectric grease to all ground terminals and exposed connectors during routine maintenance
Routinely check for cracked or brittle insulation on wiring harnesses, especially near headlights and taillights
Store a small kit with spare ring terminals, butt connectors, and heat shrink tubing in your glove box for emergency repairs
Always use automotive-grade wire and terminals rated for at least 105°C (221°F) and tinned for corrosion resistance

CHAPTER 11: TROUBLESHOOTING COMMON ENGINE PROBLEMS

No-start diagnosis and starter relay replacement

THE CAR MAINTENANCE AND REPAIR BIBLE

Materials and Tools

- Digital multimeter (auto-ranging, minimum 10A/600V, with continuity and voltage modes)
- 3/8-inch drive ratchet and socket set (8mm, 10mm, 12mm sockets)
- Combination wrenches (8mm, 10mm, 12mm)
- Insulated screwdriver set (Phillips #2, flathead 1/4-inch tip)
- Replacement starter relay (OEM or high-quality aftermarket, matched to vehicle year/make/model)
- Battery terminal puller (if terminals are corroded or seized)
- Battery post and terminal cleaner (wire brush, 4-in-1 tool)
- Nitrile gloves (5–7 mil thickness)
- Safety glasses (ANSI Z87.1 rated)
- Shop light or headlamp (LED, 200+ lumens)
- Clean microfiber towels (16x16 inch, lint-free, set of 2)
- Dielectric grease (0.5 oz tube)
- Owner's manual (for relay location and fuse box diagram)
- Service manual or wiring diagram (for starter circuit and relay pinout)
- Jumper wire with alligator clips (16 AWG, 12-inch length, for bypass testing)
- Torque wrench (5–20 ft-lb range)

Step-by-step instructions

1. Park the vehicle on a flat, paved surface; engage the parking brake and turn off the ignition
2. Open the hood and put on nitrile gloves and safety glasses for protection
3. Inspect the battery terminals for corrosion or looseness; clean with a wire brush and tighten as needed
4. Set the digital multimeter to DC voltage (20V range); connect the red probe to the battery positive terminal and the black probe to the negative terminal
5. Record the battery voltage; a healthy battery should read 12.4–12.7V with the engine off
6. Turn the ignition key to the "Start" position and observe the multimeter; if voltage drops below 10.5V, suspect a weak battery—charge or replace before proceeding
7. Locate the starter relay using the owner's manual or fuse box diagram; common locations include the under-hood fuse/relay box or driver's side kick panel
8. With the ignition off, remove the starter relay by pulling it straight up or using a relay puller tool if access is tight
9. Inspect the relay terminals for corrosion, discoloration, or bent pins; clean with a microfiber towel if needed
10. Set the multimeter to continuity mode; test the relay coil by probing the control terminals (typically pins 85 and 86)—a good relay should show 50–120 ohms resistance
11. Test the relay switch by probing the output terminals (typically pins 30 and 87); there should be no continuity with the relay removed
12. Insert a jumper wire between the

THE CAR MAINTENANCE AND REPAIR BIBLE

relay socket terminals for the output circuit (30 and 87) to bypass the relay; with the ignition in "Run," the starter should engage—if so, the relay is faulty

13. If the starter does not engage with the jumper, check for voltage at the relay socket's control terminal (pin 86) while turning the key to "Start"; should read battery voltage (12V+)
14. If no voltage is present at the control terminal, trace the circuit back to the ignition switch or neutral safety switch using the wiring diagram
15. If voltage is present and the starter still does not engage, check for voltage at the starter solenoid terminal while cranking; if absent, suspect a wiring fault or bad starter
16. Install the new starter relay by aligning the pins and pressing firmly into the socket until fully seated
17. Apply a thin layer of dielectric grease to the relay terminals before installation to prevent corrosion
18. Reconnect any covers or panels removed during access
19. Attempt to start the vehicle; verify that the engine cranks and starts normally
20. Clean the work area and dispose of the old relay according to local regulations

Illustrations and diagrams

Diagram of typical under-hood fuse/relay box layout with starter relay location highlighted
Schematic of starter circuit showing battery, ignition switch, relay, and starter motor connections
Step-by-step visual of relay removal, continuity testing, and installation
Multimeter probe placement for voltage and continuity checks at relay socket

Practical expert tips

Always test battery health and terminal tightness before diagnosing starter circuit issues; many no-starts are due to poor battery connections
Mark the date and mileage of relay replacement in your maintenance log or on a sticker inside the fuse box cover
Use a shop light to inspect relay sockets for signs of heat damage or melted plastic, which indicate high resistance or poor contact
If the relay clicks but the starter does not engage, tap the starter motor lightly with a rubber mallet while cranking—if it starts, the starter is likely failing
For intermittent no-starts, swap the starter relay with another identical relay (such as the horn or A/C relay) to confirm diagnosis before purchasing a new part

Troubleshooting techniques

If the starter relay tests good but the vehicle still won't crank, check the neutral safety switch (automatic) or clutch pedal switch (manual) for proper operation
If the relay clicks but no voltage reaches the starter, inspect the wiring harness for broken, frayed, or corroded wires between the relay and starter solenoid
If the starter engages but cranks slowly, test for excessive voltage drop across the main battery cables and ground straps; replace any cable with more than 0.2V drop under load
If the relay repeatedly fails, check

for oil or water intrusion in the fuse/relay box and repair any leaks or seals as needed

If the starter runs continuously after releasing the key, suspect a sticking relay or ignition switch—replace both if necessary

Security and preventive maintenance

Inspect and clean battery terminals and starter relay connections every 12 months or before long trips

Apply dielectric grease to all relay and fuse terminals during routine maintenance to prevent corrosion

Routinely check for loose or damaged wiring in the starter circuit, especially after engine work or off-road driving

Store a spare starter relay and a jumper wire in your glove box for emergency roadside repairs

Always use relays that meet OEM specifications for current rating and pin configuration to ensure safe and reliable starter operation

Cylinder misfire diagnosis with spark plug and ignition coil service

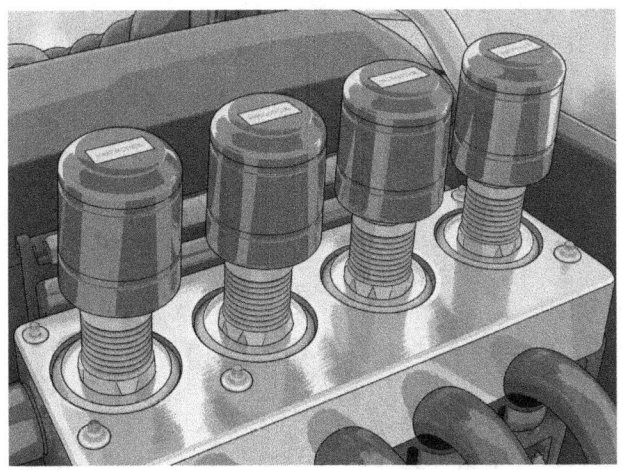

Materials and Tools

- Digital OBD-II scanner (with live data and freeze frame capability)
- 3/8-inch drive ratchet and extension (6-inch)
- Spark plug socket (5/8-inch or 9/16-inch, magnetic or rubber insert)
- Torque wrench (inch-pound, 120–240 in-lb range)
- Feeler gauge set (0.020–0.045 inch range)
- Replacement spark plugs (OEM-specified, copper/iridium/platinum as required)
- Replacement ignition coil(s) (OEM or high-quality aftermarket, matched to vehicle year/make/model)
- Dielectric grease (0.5 oz tube)
- Compressed air canister or air compressor with blow gun
- Anti-seize compound (nickel-based, 0.5 oz tube, if recommended by manufacturer)
- Nitrile gloves (5–7 mil thickness)
- Safety glasses (ANSI Z87.1 rated)
- Shop light or headlamp (LED, 200+ lumens)
- Clean microfiber towels (16x16 inch, lint-free, set of 2)
- Small wire brush (brass, 4-inch handle)
- Multimeter (for coil resistance testing, 10MΩ input impedance)
- Owner's manual and service manual (for firing order, plug gap, and torque specs)
- Permanent marker (for coil and wire labeling)
- Vacuum gauge (optional, for advanced diagnostics)

Step-by-step instructions

1. Park the vehicle on a flat, paved surface; engage the parking brake and turn off the ignition

2. Open the hood and allow the engine to cool for at least 30 minutes to prevent burns from hot components
3. Connect the OBD-II scanner to the diagnostic port under the dashboard; turn the ignition to "On" (engine off) and read stored codes
4. Record any misfire codes (P0301–P0308) and note the affected cylinder(s); use live data to confirm misfire frequency and cylinder number
5. With the engine off, disconnect the negative battery terminal using a 10mm wrench to prevent accidental shorts
6. Remove any engine covers or air intake ducts blocking access to the ignition coils and spark plugs using the appropriate sockets and screwdrivers
7. Label each ignition coil and corresponding wire/connector with a permanent marker to ensure correct reinstallation
8. Use compressed air to blow away debris around the spark plug wells to prevent dirt from falling into the cylinders
9. Disconnect the electrical connector from the ignition coil by pressing the release tab and gently pulling straight off
10. Remove the ignition coil mounting bolt (typically 8mm or 10mm) with a ratchet and extension; carefully pull the coil straight up and out
11. Inspect the ignition coil for cracks, carbon tracking, or oil contamination; set aside for testing or replacement
12. Insert the spark plug socket and extension into the well; turn counterclockwise to remove the spark plug
13. Inspect the spark plug for fouling, oil deposits, worn electrodes, or cracked porcelain; compare to service manual photos for diagnosis
14. Measure the spark plug gap with a feeler gauge; adjust only if specified by the manufacturer (most iridium/platinum plugs are pre-gapped)
15. Clean reusable plugs with a brass wire brush if not replacing; if replacing, apply a thin layer of anti-seize compound to the threads only if recommended by the manufacturer
16. Install the new or cleaned spark plug by hand, turning clockwise until finger-tight; use a torque wrench to tighten to the specified value (typically 18–25 ft-lb for aluminum heads, 25–30 ft-lb for cast iron)
17. Apply a small amount of dielectric grease to the inside of the ignition coil boot to prevent moisture intrusion and ease future removal
18. Reinstall the ignition coil, aligning it with the spark plug and pressing firmly until fully seated; reinstall and tighten the mounting bolt to manufacturer specs (typically 70–90 in-lb)
19. Reconnect the electrical connector to the ignition coil until it clicks securely
20. Repeat the process for any additional misfiring cylinders or as part of a full tune-up
21. Reinstall any engine covers or air intake ducts removed earlier
22. Reconnect the negative battery terminal and tighten securely
23. Start the engine and monitor for smooth idle; use the OBD-II scanner to clear codes and verify that no

new misfire codes appear during a test drive

Illustrations and diagrams

Diagram of typical ignition coil and spark plug layout for inline-4 and V6 engines
Cross-section of spark plug showing common fouling types and wear patterns
Step-by-step visual of coil removal, spark plug extraction, inspection, and reinstallation
Schematic of ignition system with test points for coil resistance and plug gap

Practical expert tips

Always use spark plugs specified by the manufacturer for heat range and electrode material; mismatched plugs can cause persistent misfires
If a misfire code returns after plug and coil replacement, swap the suspect coil to another cylinder and see if the misfire follows—this isolates a bad coil
Mark the date and mileage of spark plug and coil service in your maintenance log or on a sticker under the hood
For engines with deep plug wells, use a magnetic or rubber-insert socket to prevent dropping plugs into the engine bay
If oil is present on the plug or coil, inspect valve cover gaskets and plug tube seals for leaks and replace as needed

Troubleshooting techniques

If the misfire persists after plug and coil replacement, use a multimeter to check coil primary and secondary resistance against service manual specs
Use the OBD-II scanner's live data to monitor misfire counts at idle and under load; intermittent misfires may indicate wiring or injector issues
If multiple adjacent cylinders misfire, check for vacuum leaks at the intake manifold or gasket near those cylinders
For random misfires (P0300), inspect fuel pressure, injector operation, and engine compression
If the engine runs rough only when cold, suspect a failing coolant temperature sensor or intake air leak

Security and preventive maintenance

Replace spark plugs every 30,000–100,000 miles depending on type (copper, platinum, iridium) and manufacturer recommendations
Inspect ignition coils and plug boots for cracks or carbon tracking every 12 months or 12,000 miles
Apply dielectric grease to all coil boots during routine maintenance to prevent moisture-related misfires
Routinely check for oil leaks around the valve cover and plug wells, especially after high-mileage or older vehicles
Store a spare spark plug and coil in your glove box or trunk for emergency roadside repairs if your vehicle is prone to ignition issues

Engine overheating diagnosis with thermostat and water pump replacement

THE CAR MAINTENANCE AND REPAIR BIBLE

Materials and Tools

- Digital infrared thermometer (range: -58°F to 1022°F, accuracy ±2°F)
- OBD-II scanner (with live data coolant temp monitoring)
- Coolant system pressure tester (0–30 psi gauge, compatible with radiator cap)
- Replacement thermostat (OEM-specified temperature, typically 180–195°F)
- Replacement water pump (OEM or high-quality aftermarket, matched to vehicle year/make/model)
- New radiator cap (OEM pressure rating, usually 13–16 psi)
- Pre-mixed engine coolant (50/50 ethylene glycol, phosphate-free, silicate-free, quantity per owner's manual, typically 1–2 gallons)
- Distilled water (1 gallon, for flushing)
- Gasket scraper (1-inch blade, plastic or brass)
- Torque wrench (inch-pound and foot-pound, 10–80 ft-lb range)
- 3/8-inch drive ratchet and socket set (8mm, 10mm, 12mm, 13mm, 14mm, 15mm sockets)
- Combination wrenches (10mm, 12mm, 14mm)
- Large drain pan (at least 2-gallon capacity)
- Funnel (wide-mouth, coolant-safe)
- Nitrile gloves (5–7 mil thickness)
- Safety glasses (ANSI Z87.1 rated)
- Shop towels (lint-free, 16x16 inch)
- Gasket sealant (non-hardening, if specified by manufacturer)
- New thermostat gasket or O-ring (OEM specified)
- New water pump gasket or O-ring (OEM specified)
- Pliers (for hose clamps)
- Flathead screwdriver (1/4-inch tip)
- Service manual (for torque specs, belt routing, and component locations)
- Jack and jack stands (3-ton capacity, if undercarriage access is needed)
- Coolant spill absorbent (granular or pads, for cleanup)

Step-by-step instructions

1. Park the vehicle on a flat, paved surface; engage the parking brake and allow the engine to cool for at least 1 hour to avoid burns from hot coolant
2. Open the hood and put on nitrile gloves and safety glasses for protection
3. Place a large drain pan under the radiator drain plug or lower radiator hose; use pliers to loosen the hose clamp or open the drain valve, allowing coolant to drain completely (expect 1–2 gallons)
4. Remove the radiator cap to speed draining; inspect the cap for cracks, worn seals, or corrosion—replace if any defects are found
5. Use an OBD-II scanner to check for stored engine temperature codes (P0125, P0217, etc.) and monitor live coolant temperature data; note if the engine exceeds 220°F during

operation

6. With the engine off, use a digital infrared thermometer to check temperature differences between the upper and lower radiator hoses after warm-up; a difference greater than 30°F may indicate a stuck thermostat

7. Pressurize the cooling system with a pressure tester to the radiator cap's rated pressure (typically 13–16 psi); inspect for leaks at hoses, radiator, water pump, and thermostat housing

8. Locate the thermostat housing by following the upper radiator hose to the engine; remove any engine covers or air intake ducts blocking access using the appropriate sockets and screwdrivers

9. Use a ratchet and socket to remove the thermostat housing bolts (typically 10mm or 12mm); gently pry off the housing and note the orientation of the old thermostat

10. Remove the old thermostat and gasket; clean the mating surfaces with a gasket scraper and shop towels until free of old gasket material and debris

11. Install the new thermostat with the spring side facing the engine; ensure the jiggle valve (if present) is positioned at the 12 o'clock position for air bleeding

12. Place the new gasket or O-ring in the groove; apply a thin layer of non-hardening gasket sealant if specified by the manufacturer

13. Reinstall the thermostat housing and torque the bolts to the manufacturer's specification (typically 8–12 ft-lb)

14. If water pump replacement is needed, remove the serpentine belt by rotating the tensioner with a wrench (refer to belt routing diagram); remove any pulleys or brackets obstructing the pump

15. Use a ratchet and socket to remove the water pump mounting bolts (typically 10mm, 12mm, or 14mm); gently tap the pump with a rubber mallet to break the seal and remove it

16. Clean the engine block mating surface with a gasket scraper and shop towels; ensure no old gasket material remains

17. Install the new water pump with a new gasket or O-ring; apply gasket sealant if specified; align the pump and hand-tighten bolts before torquing to manufacturer's specification (typically 15–22 ft-lb)

18. Reinstall any pulleys, brackets, and the serpentine belt according to the belt routing diagram; ensure proper belt tension

19. Reconnect any hoses and clamps removed during disassembly; double-check all fasteners for tightness

20. Close the radiator drain plug or reattach the lower hose; use a funnel to refill the system with pre-mixed coolant to the "Full" mark on the reservoir

21. Start the engine and let it idle with the radiator cap off; monitor coolant level and add as needed while watching for air bubbles (burping the system)

22. Once the thermostat opens (upper hose becomes hot), top off coolant, reinstall the radiator cap, and check for leaks

23. Use the OBD-II scanner and infrared thermometer to confirm normal operating temperature (typically 190–210°F) and even hose temperatures

24. Clean up any spilled coolant with absorbent and dispose of old coolant at a recycling center

Illustrations and diagrams

Diagram of typical cooling system layout showing radiator, thermostat, water pump, and hose routing
Cross-section of thermostat installation with correct orientation and jiggle valve position
Step-by-step visual of water pump removal, gasket cleaning, and new pump installation
Schematic of serpentine belt routing and tensioner location

Practical expert tips

Always use pre-mixed, manufacturer-approved coolant to prevent mineral deposits and electrolysis in the cooling system
Mark the date and mileage of thermostat and water pump replacement in your maintenance log or on a sticker under the hood
If the old water pump shows signs of shaft play, noisy bearings, or coolant stains at the weep hole, replace it even if not leaking
Use a digital thermometer to check for hot spots on the radiator surface, which may indicate internal blockage
When burping the system, set the heater to maximum to help purge air from the heater core

Troubleshooting techniques

If overheating persists after thermostat and water pump replacement, check for a clogged radiator, collapsed hoses, or a faulty radiator fan
If the engine overheats only at idle, suspect a non-functioning electric fan or faulty fan relay
If coolant loss continues with no visible leaks, inspect for head gasket failure (look for white exhaust smoke, milky oil, or bubbles in the coolant)
If the new thermostat fails prematurely, verify that the cooling system is free of rust and debris, and that the correct temperature rating was used
If the serpentine belt squeals after reassembly, check for proper belt alignment and tension; replace the belt if cracked or glazed

Security and preventive maintenance

Inspect coolant level and condition every 3,000 miles or at every oil change; top off with pre-mixed coolant as needed
Replace the thermostat and water pump every 60,000–100,000 miles or as recommended by the manufacturer
Flush the cooling system with distilled water every 2–3 years to remove scale and prevent corrosion
Check all hoses for swelling, cracks, or soft spots during routine maintenance and replace as needed
Store a spare radiator cap and a gallon of pre-mixed coolant in your trunk for emergency roadside repairs

Rough idle troubleshooting with intake manifold and vacuum leak repair

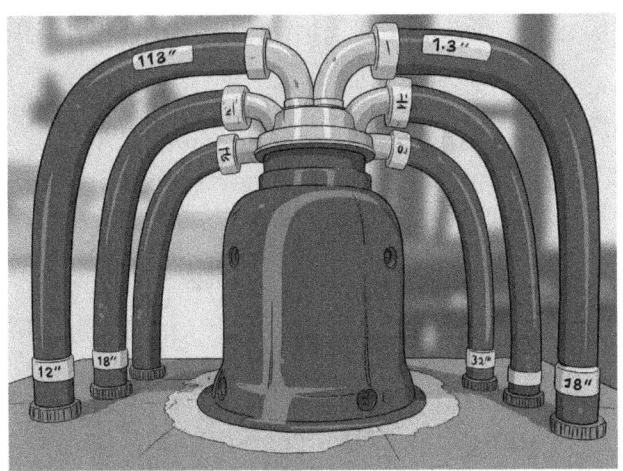

Materials and Tools

- Smoke machine leak detector (automotive, 0.5–5 psi output, with mineral oil)
- Digital vacuum gauge (0–30 inHg, ±0.1 inHg accuracy)
- Mechanic's stethoscope (with probe tip)
- Carburetor or brake cleaner spray (non-chlorinated, 12–16 oz can)
- OBD-II scanner (with live data capability)
- 3/8-inch drive ratchet and socket set (8mm, 10mm, 12mm, 13mm, 14mm)
- Flathead screwdriver (1/4-inch tip, 6-inch shaft)
- Replacement vacuum hoses (3/16-inch, 1/4-inch, and 3/8-inch ID, 3 ft each, fuel-rated)
- Hose clamps (worm gear, 1/4-inch to 1/2-inch range, stainless steel)
- Intake manifold gasket set (OEM specified, multi-layer steel or composite)
- Torque wrench (inch-pound and foot-pound, 10–80 ft-lb range)
- Nitrile gloves (5–7 mil thickness)
- Safety glasses (ANSI Z87.1 rated)
- Shop towels (lint-free, 16x16 inch)
- Flashlight (LED, 200+ lumens)
- Service manual (for torque specs, vacuum routing, and manifold removal procedure)
- Replacement intake manifold bolts (if TTY or corroded)
- Gasket scraper (1-inch blade, plastic or brass)
- Shop vacuum (for debris removal)
- Permanent marker (for hose and connector labeling)
- Small mirror (2-inch, telescoping handle)

Step-by-step instructions

1. Park the vehicle on a flat, paved surface; engage the parking brake and allow the engine to cool for at least 30 minutes
2. Open the hood and put on nitrile gloves and safety glasses for protection
3. Connect the OBD-II scanner to the diagnostic port; turn the ignition to "On" (engine off) and check for stored codes (P0171, P0174, P0300, etc.); note any fuel trim or misfire data
4. Start the engine and observe idle quality; if rough, use the digital vacuum gauge to measure intake manifold vacuum at a dedicated port —normal idle vacuum should be 17–22 inHg; readings below 15 inHg or fluctuating indicate a leak
5. With the engine idling, spray carburetor or brake cleaner in short bursts around the intake manifold gasket, vacuum hoses, throttle body base, and PCV connections; listen for RPM changes, which indicate a leak at the sprayed location
6. Use a smoke machine to introduce smoke into a vacuum port or the brake booster hose; observe for smoke escaping around the intake manifold, hose connections, or gaskets—use a flashlight and small mirror to inspect hard-to-see

areas

7. Mark all vacuum hoses and electrical connectors with a permanent marker for reassembly; photograph hose routing for reference

8. If a vacuum hose is cracked, brittle, or loose, remove it with a flathead screwdriver or by gently twisting and pulling; cut a new hose to length and install with new clamps, ensuring a snug fit

9. If the intake manifold gasket is leaking, disconnect the negative battery terminal and remove all hoses, sensors, and brackets attached to the manifold using the appropriate sockets and screwdrivers

10. Remove the intake manifold bolts in the reverse order of the tightening sequence (refer to the service manual); lift the manifold off carefully, avoiding damage to mating surfaces

11. Use a gasket scraper and shop towels to clean the cylinder head and manifold mating surfaces until free of old gasket material and debris; use a shop vacuum to remove any loose particles

12. Place the new intake manifold gasket(s) onto the cylinder head, aligning all bolt holes and ports; if specified, apply a thin layer of RTV sealant at the corners or joints

13. Lower the intake manifold into position, ensuring proper alignment; hand-thread all bolts before tightening

14. Torque the intake manifold bolts in the specified sequence and to the manufacturer's torque specification (typically 15–22 ft-lb for aluminum manifolds, 22–30 ft-lb for cast iron)

15. Reconnect all hoses, sensors, and brackets, matching the labels and photos taken earlier; replace any damaged connectors or clamps

16. Reinstall the negative battery terminal and tighten securely

17. Start the engine and monitor idle quality; use the OBD-II scanner to check for normal fuel trims (±5%) and absence of vacuum-related codes

18. Recheck vacuum gauge readings; confirm stable idle vacuum within the normal range

19. Test drive the vehicle and monitor for smooth idle and proper engine response

Illustrations and diagrams

Diagram of typical intake manifold and vacuum hose routing for inline-4 and V6 engines
Cross-section of intake manifold gasket installation with torque sequence
Step-by-step visual of smoke machine leak detection and carburetor cleaner spray test
Schematic of vacuum gauge connection points and normal/abnormal readings

Practical expert tips

Always use OEM-specified intake manifold gaskets for best sealing and durability; avoid cheap aftermarket gaskets that may not fit precisely
Replace all vacuum hoses over 10 years old, even if they appear intact, as internal cracking is common
Mark the date and mileage of intake manifold and vacuum hose service in your maintenance log or on a sticker under the hood
If the intake manifold bolts are

torque-to-yield (TTY), always replace them with new ones to prevent improper clamping force
Use a mechanic's stethoscope to pinpoint hissing sounds that may indicate small vacuum leaks in hard-to-reach areas

Troubleshooting techniques

If rough idle persists after vacuum leak repair, check for stuck open EGR valve, faulty PCV valve, or intake air leaks downstream of the mass airflow sensor
If the engine idles high after repair, inspect for disconnected or misrouted vacuum hoses and ensure the throttle body gasket is properly sealed
If fuel trims remain high (over +10%) after repairs, test for exhaust leaks near the upstream O2 sensor or a faulty mass airflow sensor
If the engine stalls when spraying cleaner, the leak may be large or the cleaner is entering the intake directly—reinspect gasket alignment and hose connections
If the smoke machine reveals no leaks but idle is still rough, perform a compression test to rule out internal engine issues

Security and preventive maintenance

Inspect all vacuum hoses and intake manifold gaskets every 12 months or 12,000 miles for signs of wear, cracking, or leaks
Replace the PCV valve and associated hoses every 30,000–50,000 miles to prevent vacuum-related idle issues
Use only fuel-rated vacuum hoses to prevent softening and collapse from engine heat and oil vapors
Keep a can of carburetor cleaner and a length of spare vacuum hose in your trunk for emergency roadside diagnostics
Log all repairs and parts replaced to track maintenance intervals and identify recurring issues early

4 TROUBLESHOOTING COMMON ENGINE PROBLEMS

Cold and hard-start diagnosis — fuel pump, filter and pressure test

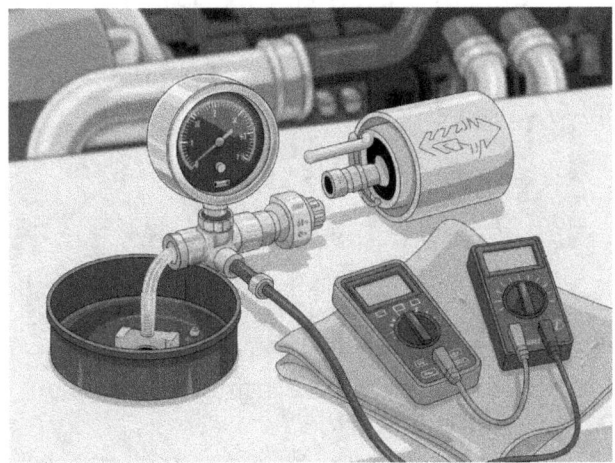

Materials and Tools

- Fuel pressure gauge kit (0–100 psi range, with Schrader valve adapter and bleed hose)
- Digital multimeter (10A DC current range, 0.1V accuracy)
- OBD-II scanner (live data and freeze frame capability)
- Replacement fuel filter (OEM-specified, in-line or in-tank type as per vehicle)
- Replacement fuel pump (OEM or high-quality aftermarket, matched to vehicle year/make/model)
- Fuel line disconnect tool set (3/8-

inch, 5/16-inch, and 1/2-inch sizes)
- Nitrile gloves (5–7 mil thickness)
- Safety glasses (ANSI Z87.1 rated)
- Shop towels (lint-free, 16x16 inch)
- Catch pan (minimum 1-gallon capacity, fuel-resistant)
- Ratchet and socket set (8mm, 10mm, 12mm, 13mm, 14mm)
- Flathead screwdriver (1/4-inch tip)
- Service manual (for fuel system specs, filter location, and pressure values)
- Fire extinguisher (Class B, rated for flammable liquids)
- Jack and jack stands (3-ton capacity, if undercarriage access is needed)
- Fuel-safe hose clamps (1/4-inch to 1/2-inch range, stainless steel)
- Permanent marker (for hose and connector labeling)

Step-by-step instructions

1. Park the vehicle outdoors on a flat, paved surface away from open flames or sparks; engage the parking brake and disconnect the negative battery terminal to prevent accidental ignition
2. Put on nitrile gloves and safety glasses for protection; keep a fire extinguisher within reach
3. Locate the fuel pressure test port (Schrader valve) on the fuel rail; if not present, consult the service manual for the correct tap-in point or use a T-adapter at the fuel filter
4. Attach the fuel pressure gauge securely to the test port; route the bleed hose into a catch pan to safely collect any fuel released during testing
5. Reconnect the negative battery terminal; cycle the ignition key to the "On" position (engine off) to prime the fuel pump; observe the gauge for initial pressure build-up (should reach 35–60 psi for most gasoline engines—verify exact spec in service manual)
6. Attempt to start the engine; note the fuel pressure during cranking and after the engine starts—pressure should remain steady within 5 psi of the spec; a drop below spec indicates a weak pump or clogged filter
7. With the engine idling, monitor the gauge for at least 2 minutes; pressure should remain stable—fluctuations or rapid drops suggest a failing pump, leaking injector, or faulty pressure regulator
8. Turn off the engine and observe the gauge; pressure should hold for at least 5 minutes—if it drops more than 5 psi, check for leaking injectors, check valve failure in the pump, or external leaks at fittings
9. If pressure is low, locate the fuel filter (typically along the frame rail or near the tank for in-line types); use the correct disconnect tool to release the fuel lines, catching any spilled fuel in the pan
10. Remove the old filter, noting the flow direction marked on the housing; install the new filter with new hose clamps, ensuring a tight, leak-free fit
11. If pressure remains low after filter replacement, test the fuel pump electrical circuit: use a digital multimeter to check for 12V at the pump connector with the ignition "On"; measure current draw (should be 4–8A for most pumps—refer to service manual)
12. If voltage or current is low, inspect the fuel pump relay, fuse, and wiring for corrosion or loose connections; replace as needed

13. If the pump receives proper voltage/current but pressure is still low, replace the fuel pump: support the fuel tank with a jack, disconnect fuel lines and electrical connectors, remove tank straps, and lower the tank to access the pump module
14. Remove the pump retaining ring or bolts, extract the old pump, and install the new unit with a fresh O-ring or gasket; reassemble the tank, reconnect all lines, and refill with fuel if needed
15. Reconnect the battery, cycle the ignition to prime the system, and repeat the pressure test to confirm normal operation
16. Use the OBD-II scanner to check for stored codes (P0087, P0230, P0191, etc.) and monitor live fuel pressure data if supported; clear codes after successful repair

Illustrations and diagrams

Diagram of typical fuel system layout showing tank, pump, filter, lines, and fuel rail with test port
Cross-section of in-line and in-tank fuel filter installation with flow direction
Step-by-step visual of fuel pressure gauge connection and reading interpretation
Schematic of fuel pump electrical circuit with relay, fuse, and connector test points

Practical expert tips

Always relieve fuel system pressure before disconnecting any lines by depressing the Schrader valve with a rag or using the gauge's bleed hose
Mark the date and mileage of fuel filter and pump replacement in your maintenance log or on a sticker near the fuel tank
Use only OEM or high-quality aftermarket fuel filters and pumps to ensure proper flow and longevity
If the vehicle is hard to start only after sitting overnight, suspect a leaking injector or faulty pump check valve causing pressure bleed-down
When replacing the fuel pump, always install a new tank seal or O-ring to prevent vapor leaks and EVAP system codes

Troubleshooting techniques

If fuel pressure is within spec but the engine is still hard to start, check for weak spark, low battery voltage, or faulty crankshaft position sensor
If the engine starts but stalls immediately, verify that the fuel pump relay is not dropping out after initial prime (test with a jumper wire if needed)
If the fuel pressure gauge needle vibrates or pulses, suspect a failing pressure regulator or air in the fuel lines—bleed the system and retest
If the fuel pump is noisy (whining or buzzing), check for restricted filter, low fuel level, or contaminated fuel; replace as needed
If the OBD-II scanner shows fuel trim codes (P0171/P0174) after repairs, inspect for vacuum leaks or intake air leaks affecting mixture

Security and preventive maintenance

Replace the fuel filter every 30,000–50,000 miles or as recommended by the manufacturer, especially if using ethanol-blended fuels
Inspect fuel lines and connections

for leaks, cracks, or corrosion at every oil change; replace any damaged sections immediately
Keep the fuel tank at least 1/4 full to prevent pump overheating and premature failure
Use only top-tier gasoline to minimize injector and filter clogging from deposits
Log all fuel system repairs and pressure test results to track trends and catch issues before they cause breakdowns

Excessive exhaust smoke diagnosis — oil burning, coolant leak and injector check

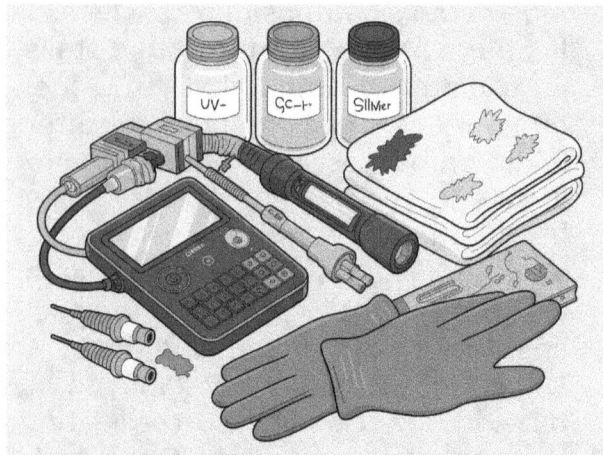

Materials and Tools

- OBD-II scanner (live data and freeze frame capability)
- Compression tester (gasoline: 0–300 psi, diesel: 0–600 psi, with adapters)
- Cylinder leak-down tester (0–100 psi, dual gauge)
- Cooling system pressure tester (0–30 psi, with radiator and reservoir adapters)
- UV dye kit (engine oil and coolant compatible, includes dye and UV flashlight, 365–395nm)
- Fuel injector balance tester (for multiport systems, 0–100 psi gauge, pulse controller)
- Infrared thermometer (–58°F to 1022°F, ±2% accuracy)
- White shop towels (lint-free, 16x16 inch)
- Nitrile gloves (5–7 mil thickness)
- Safety glasses (ANSI Z87.1 rated)
- Oil catch pan (minimum 2-gallon capacity)
- Spark plug socket (5/8-inch or 13/16-inch, 3/8-inch drive)
- Ratchet and socket set (8mm, 10mm, 12mm, 13mm, 14mm)
- Flathead screwdriver (1/4-inch tip)
- Service manual (for engine specs, injector resistance, and test procedures)
- Clean glass jars (3, 8 oz each, for injector flow test)
- Permanent marker (for labeling samples)
- Small inspection mirror (2-inch, telescoping handle)

Step-by-step instructions

1. Park the vehicle on a flat, paved surface; engage the parking brake and allow the engine to cool for at least 30 minutes
2. Put on nitrile gloves and safety glasses for protection
3. Start the engine and observe exhaust smoke color and behavior:
4. - Blue/gray smoke: likely oil burning
5. - White smoke (persistent, sweet odor): likely coolant leak
6. - Black smoke: likely excess fuel/injector issue
7. Use the OBD-II scanner to check for stored codes (P0172, P0175, P0300, P0301–P0308, P0217, P0128, etc.) and note freeze frame data

8. For blue/gray smoke (oil burning):
9. - Remove spark plugs using the correct socket; inspect for oily deposits or wetness
10. - Perform a compression test on all cylinders; record readings (gasoline: 120-210 psi, diesel: 350-500 psi; variation between cylinders should be less than 10%)
11. - If low compression is found, perform a cylinder leak-down test at TDC; listen for air escaping from oil filler (rings), intake (valves), or exhaust (valves)
12. - Add UV dye to engine oil, run engine for 10 minutes, then inspect valve cover, head gasket, and turbo seals with UV flashlight for leaks
13. For white smoke (coolant leak):
14. - Check coolant level and inspect for oil contamination (milky appearance)
15. - Install cooling system pressure tester; pressurize to cap rating (typically 13-16 psi for most cars) and observe for pressure drop over 10 minutes
16. - Inspect exhaust tip and spark plugs for coolant residue (white crust or steam)
17. - Add UV dye to coolant, run engine, and inspect head gasket area, intake manifold, and heater core connections with UV flashlight
18. - Use infrared thermometer to compare exhaust manifold temps; a cold cylinder may indicate coolant ingestion
19. For black smoke (injector/fuel issue):
20. - Use OBD-II scanner to monitor fuel trims and injector pulse width; high negative trims or long pulse width indicate excess fuel
21. - Perform injector balance test: connect fuel pressure gauge, disable ignition, and pulse each injector for equal duration; pressure drop per injector should be within 1-2 psi of each other
22. - Remove suspect injectors and test spray pattern into labeled glass jars; look for uneven flow or dripping
23. - Check injector resistance with a multimeter (typical: 12-16 ohms for gasoline, 1-3 ohms for diesel; refer to service manual)
24. Record all findings and label any fluid samples for further analysis

Illustrations and diagrams

Diagram of exhaust smoke color chart with causes (oil, coolant, fuel)
Cross-section of cylinder showing oil control ring failure and coolant leak paths
Step-by-step visual of compression and leak-down tester setup
Schematic of injector balance test with fuel pressure gauge and pulse controller

Practical expert tips

Always diagnose exhaust smoke with the engine at full operating temperature; condensation can cause temporary white smoke on cold start
Use a clean white shop towel to catch exhaust at idle—oil burning leaves blue/gray stains, coolant leaves a sweet odor and white residue, excess fuel leaves black soot
Mark the date and mileage of any injector, gasket, or seal replacement in your maintenance log
If UV dye is used, clean all traces after diagnosis to avoid future confusion
For turbocharged engines, inspect

turbo oil seals and intercooler for oil accumulation if blue smoke is present

Troubleshooting techniques

If compression is low but leak-down is normal, suspect worn piston rings or cylinder wall glazing
If cooling system pressure drops with no external leaks, suspect head gasket failure or cracked cylinder head/block
If black smoke persists after injector replacement, check for faulty mass airflow sensor or stuck open EGR valve
If white smoke only appears at startup and disappears, suspect minor head gasket seepage or condensation, but monitor coolant loss
If oil level rises and smells of fuel, suspect leaking injector washing down cylinder walls

Security and preventive maintenance

Change engine oil and filter every 5,000–7,500 miles to minimize oil burning and sludge buildup
Replace coolant every 2–5 years (per manufacturer) to prevent corrosion and head gasket failure
Use only OEM or high-quality injectors and seals to ensure proper fuel delivery and prevent leaks
Inspect PCV valve and system every 15,000 miles to prevent excessive crankcase pressure and oil consumption
Log all smoke-related diagnoses and repairs to track recurring issues and catch early signs of engine wear

Engine knock and ping troubleshooting — knock sensor, timing and octane fixes

Materials and Tools

- OBD-II scanner (live data and freeze frame capability)
- Digital timing light (advance/retard function, 0–60° range)
- Knock sensor socket (22mm deep, 3/8-inch drive, insulated)
- Multimeter (0.1V accuracy, continuity and resistance modes)
- Fuel octane booster (minimum 104+ rating, 12 oz bottle)
- Service manual (for timing specs, knock sensor location, torque values)
- Torque wrench (inch-pound and foot-pound, 5–80 ft-lb range)
- Mechanic's stethoscope (for pinpointing engine noises)
- 3/8-inch drive ratchet and extension set (3–12 inch)
- Dielectric grease (for sensor connectors)
- Shop towels (lint-free, 16x16 inch)
- Nitrile gloves (5–7 mil thickness)
- Safety glasses (ANSI Z87.1 rated)
- Permanent marker (for marking timing marks)

- Chalk or white paint pen (for timing mark visibility)

Step-by-step instructions

1. Park the vehicle on a flat, paved surface; engage the parking brake and allow the engine to cool for at least 30 minutes
2. Put on nitrile gloves and safety glasses for protection
3. Connect the OBD-II scanner to the diagnostic port; check for stored codes (P0325, P0330, P0327, P0332, P0300, etc.) and note freeze frame data
4. Start the engine and listen for knocking or pinging sounds using a mechanic's stethoscope; focus on the cylinder head and block area
5. If knock is present, add a full bottle (12 oz) of 104+ octane booster to a nearly empty tank, then fill with 10 gallons of premium gasoline (91–93 octane); test drive for 10 miles and monitor for reduction in knock
6. If knock persists, locate the knock sensor (typically threaded into the engine block below the intake manifold or near the cylinder head); consult the service manual for exact location
7. Disconnect the knock sensor electrical connector; inspect for corrosion, bent pins, or oil contamination; clean with dielectric grease and reconnect
8. Use a multimeter to check knock sensor resistance (typical: 500–620 kΩ for piezoelectric sensors, 1–10 MΩ for some models—refer to service manual); replace if out of spec
9. If replacement is needed, use a 22mm knock sensor socket and torque wrench to remove the old sensor; install the new sensor to the specified torque (typically 15–25 ft-lb), ensuring the mounting surface is clean and dry
10. Mark the crankshaft pulley timing mark with chalk or a white paint pen for visibility; connect the digital timing light to the #1 spark plug wire
11. Start the engine and aim the timing light at the crankshaft pulley; compare the timing mark to the timing tab; check base timing against the service manual spec (usually 0–12° BTDC at idle for most gasoline engines)
12. If timing is advanced beyond spec, loosen the distributor hold-down bolt (if equipped) and rotate the distributor to adjust timing; retighten bolt and recheck
13. For engines with computer-controlled timing, use the OBD-II scanner to monitor live timing advance; if excessive advance is observed, check for faulty cam/crank sensors or ECM issues
14. Test drive the vehicle under moderate acceleration and uphill load; listen for knock or ping; if present, repeat timing check and verify knock sensor operation with live data (knock sensor voltage should spike during knock events)
15. If knock is eliminated with higher octane fuel or proper timing, return to regular fuel and monitor; if knock returns, continue using premium fuel or consult for possible carbon buildup or internal engine issues

Illustrations and diagrams

Diagram of engine block showing typical knock sensor locations (inline and V engines)
Cross-section of knock sensor

installation with torque spec and connector orientation
Timing mark diagram with crankshaft pulley, timing tab, and distributor adjustment
Schematic of knock sensor circuit with ECM input and signal waveform

Practical expert tips

Always use a torque wrench when installing knock sensors; overtightening can crack the sensor or block, while undertightening can cause poor signal
Mark the date and mileage of knock sensor replacement or timing adjustment in your maintenance log
If knock occurs only under heavy load or high temperatures, try switching to a higher octane fuel for several tanks to see if the issue resolves
Use only OEM or high-quality aftermarket knock sensors; cheap sensors may not detect knock accurately, leading to engine damage
If the engine is equipped with variable valve timing (VVT), check for proper oil level and quality, as VVT issues can mimic knock

Troubleshooting techniques

If knock persists after sensor replacement and timing adjustment, inspect for excessive carbon buildup on pistons and combustion chambers; use a top-end cleaner if needed
If OBD-II codes for knock sensor circuit (P0325, P0330) remain after replacement, check wiring harness for continuity and shorts to ground or power
If timing cannot be adjusted to spec, inspect the timing chain/belt for stretch or skipped teeth; replace as needed
If knock is only present with low-quality fuel, avoid gas stations with poor reputations and use top-tier gasoline
If pinging occurs only at high RPM, check for lean fuel mixture (vacuum leaks, clogged injectors, or faulty MAF sensor)

Security and preventive maintenance

Replace knock sensors every 100,000–150,000 miles or as recommended by the manufacturer
Inspect and clean sensor connectors at every major service interval (30,000 miles)
Use only the recommended octane fuel for your vehicle; avoid using lower octane than specified in the owner's manual
Log all timing adjustments, sensor replacements, and fuel changes to track trends and catch issues before they cause engine damage
Keep the engine cooling system in top condition; overheating increases the risk of knock and pre-ignition

Loss of power diagnosis — clogged catalytic converter, MAF and throttle body service

THE CAR MAINTENANCE AND REPAIR BIBLE

Materials and Tools

- OBD-II scanner (live data and freeze frame capability)
- Digital vacuum gauge (0–30 inHg, ±0.1 inHg accuracy)
- Infrared thermometer (–58°F to 1022°F, ±2% accuracy)
- Mass Air Flow (MAF) sensor cleaner (aerosol, non-residue, 12 oz can)
- Torx and security bit set (T20, T25, T30, T40)
- Phillips and flathead screwdrivers (3/16-inch and 1/4-inch tips)
- 1/4-inch drive ratchet and socket set (8mm, 10mm, 12mm)
- Throttle body cleaner (aerosol, 12 oz can, safe for coated throttle plates)
- Clean microfiber towels (16x16 inch, lint-free)
- Nitrile gloves (5–7 mil thickness)
- Safety glasses (ANSI Z87.1 rated)
- Shop vacuum (for debris removal)
- Service manual (for sensor specs, torque values, and test procedures)
- Permanent marker (for marking hoses and connectors)
- Small nylon brush (1-inch, soft bristle)
- Replacement throttle body gasket (if required by manufacturer)

Step-by-step instructions

1. Park the vehicle on a flat, paved surface; engage the parking brake and allow the engine to cool for at least 30 minutes
2. Put on nitrile gloves and safety glasses for protection
3. Connect the OBD-II scanner to the diagnostic port; check for stored codes (P0420, P0171, P0174, P0101, P0102, P2111, P2112, etc.) and note freeze frame data
4. Start the engine and observe idle quality and throttle response; note any hesitation, surging, or stalling
5. For catalytic converter diagnosis:
6. - With the engine idling, connect the digital vacuum gauge to a direct intake manifold vacuum port; record vacuum at idle (normal: 17–22 inHg)
7. - Gradually raise engine speed to 2,500 rpm and hold; observe vacuum reading—if it drops steadily by 5 inHg or more, suspect exhaust restriction
8. - With the engine fully warmed, use the infrared thermometer to measure the temperature at the front (inlet) and rear (outlet) of the catalytic converter; a healthy converter will show a 100–200°F higher outlet temp than inlet; a clogged converter may show little or no difference
9. - If a severe restriction is suspected, perform a backpressure test using a threaded port before the converter (spec: less than 1.5 psi at 2,500 rpm)
10. For MAF sensor service:
11. - Locate the MAF sensor in the intake duct between the air filter and throttle body; disconnect the negative battery terminal to prevent electrical shorts
12. - Remove the MAF sensor using the correct Torx or security bit; avoid

touching the sensor wires or film
13. - Spray the MAF sensor element thoroughly with MAF sensor cleaner (10-15 bursts); do not use compressed air or other cleaners
14. - Allow the sensor to air dry for at least 10 minutes before reinstalling; reconnect the sensor and battery terminal
15. For throttle body cleaning:
16. - Remove the intake duct from the throttle body using a screwdriver or socket; inspect for oil, carbon, or debris
17. - If equipped with an electronic throttle, do not manually force the throttle plate open; have an assistant turn the ignition to ON (engine off) to cycle the plate, or follow service manual procedure
18. - Spray throttle body cleaner onto a microfiber towel; gently wipe the throttle plate and bore, focusing on the edges and pivot points
19. - For heavy deposits, use a soft nylon brush with cleaner; avoid excessive liquid entering the intake
20. - Reinstall the intake duct and any sensors; replace the throttle body gasket if removed
21. - Start the engine and allow it to idle for 5 minutes; the idle may fluctuate as the computer relearns throttle position
22. Test drive the vehicle under moderate and full acceleration; monitor for restored power, smooth throttle response, and absence of hesitation

Illustrations and diagrams

Diagram of intake manifold vacuum gauge connection and normal vs. restricted vacuum readings
Cross-section of catalytic converter showing temperature measurement points and flow restriction
Exploded view of MAF sensor removal and cleaning procedure
Throttle body cleaning schematic with safe cleaning zones and plate position

Practical expert tips

Always use dedicated MAF sensor cleaner; brake or carburetor cleaners can damage sensitive elements
Mark all hoses and connectors with a permanent marker before removal to ensure correct reassembly
If the throttle body is heavily coated with oil, inspect the PCV system for excessive blow-by or clogging
For vehicles with drive-by-wire throttle, always follow the manufacturer's relearn procedure after cleaning to avoid idle or throttle errors
Record the date, mileage, and any codes found in your maintenance log for future reference

Troubleshooting techniques

If vacuum remains low at idle and drops further under load, check for both intake leaks and exhaust restrictions
If the MAF sensor code returns after cleaning, test the sensor's output voltage (typical: 0.5-1.0V at idle, 4.0-5.0V at wide open throttle); replace if out of spec
If throttle response is still poor after cleaning, check for throttle actuator codes and inspect wiring harness for damage
If the catalytic converter is confirmed clogged, inspect for underlying causes such as misfire, oil burning, or coolant leaks that

may have damaged the converter

Security and preventive maintenance

Replace the engine air filter every 15,000–30,000 miles to prevent MAF contamination

Clean the throttle body every 30,000 miles or as recommended by the manufacturer

Use only top-tier gasoline to minimize carbon buildup in the intake and exhaust

Inspect the PCV valve and system every 15,000 miles to reduce oil vapor entering the intake

Log all cleaning, sensor service, and converter checks to track trends and catch issues early

CHAPTER 12: 4 PREVENTIVE MAINTENANCE PROJECTS

Scheduled Maintenance Checklist and Service Interval Log

Materials and Tools

- Maintenance logbook (pre-printed or digital, with columns for date, mileage, service performed, parts used, and technician/DIY notes)
- Permanent marker (fine tip, black, for logbook entries and under-hood reminders)
- Service interval chart (vehicle-specific, printed from manufacturer or reputable source)
- Digital calendar or reminder app (with recurring event capability)
- Oil change reminder sticker (static cling, 2x2 inch, for windshield)
- Pen (medium point, black or blue, archival ink)
- Odometer reading tool (camera or smartphone for photo records)
- Maintenance record folder (letter size, with dividers for receipts and service docs)
- Laminated quick-reference checklist (8.5x11 inch, for garage wall)
- Highlighter (yellow, for marking upcoming or overdue items)
- Shop towels (lint-free, for handling logbook and documents with greasy hands)
- Nitrile gloves (5–7 mil thickness, for handling parts and paperwork)

Step-by-step instructions

1. Park the vehicle on a flat, well-lit surface; engage the parking brake and turn off the engine
2. Retrieve the owner's manual and locate the manufacturer's recommended maintenance schedule; if unavailable, print a schedule from the manufacturer's website using your vehicle's year, make, and model
3. Prepare the maintenance logbook and service interval chart; fill in the vehicle's VIN, current mileage, and date on the first page
4. Using a highlighter, mark all

critical service intervals (e.g., oil change every 5,000 miles, brake inspection every 10,000 miles, coolant flush every 60,000 miles) on the service interval chart
5. Enter the current mileage and date in the logbook; record the last completed maintenance tasks, referencing receipts or previous records if available
6. For each maintenance item, write the next due mileage and date in both the logbook and on the laminated checklist; for example, if the oil was changed at 45,000 miles, note the next change at 50,000 miles or 6 months, whichever comes first
7. Place the oil change reminder sticker on the upper left corner of the windshield, writing the next due mileage and date with a permanent marker
8. Set digital calendar reminders for each major service interval (e.g., oil, filters, brakes, transmission fluid, timing belt, spark plugs); use recurring events for regular items (e.g., every 5,000 miles or 6 months)
9. After each maintenance task, immediately update the logbook with the date, mileage, service performed, parts used (brand and part number), and any observations (e.g., "brake pads at 4mm, recommend replacement at next service")
10. File all receipts, parts packaging, and service documents in the maintenance record folder, organized by date and type of service
11. Review the laminated checklist monthly; use a highlighter to mark any items due within the next 1,000 miles or 30 days
12. Take a photo of the odometer and completed logbook entry after each major service; store digital copies in a dedicated folder on your phone or computer for backup
13. If multiple drivers use the vehicle, brief them on the location of the logbook and checklist, and instruct them to report any dashboard warning lights or unusual noises immediately
14. At the end of each year, review the logbook and service interval chart; schedule any overdue or upcoming major services, and update the laminated checklist as needed

Illustrations and diagrams

Sample maintenance logbook page with columns for date, mileage, service, parts, and notes
Example of a highlighted service interval chart with color-coded intervals (oil, brakes, fluids, etc.)
Diagram showing placement of oil change reminder sticker on windshield
Flowchart of maintenance record-keeping process from service to logbook to digital backup

Practical expert tips

Always use archival ink pens for logbook entries to prevent fading over time
Keep the maintenance logbook in the glove compartment or center console for easy access at service appointments
Use color-coded highlighters for different types of maintenance (e.g., yellow for oil, green for brakes, pink for fluids) to quickly identify

upcoming tasks

If you miss a scheduled service, perform it as soon as possible and note the reason for the delay in the logbook

When selling the vehicle, provide the complete maintenance log and folder to the buyer to increase resale value and buyer confidence

Troubleshooting techniques

If you lose track of previous maintenance, use parts receipts, oil change stickers, and online service history (if available) to reconstruct the log

For vehicles with digital service reminders, cross-check the dashboard alerts with your manual log to ensure nothing is missed

If a maintenance item is repeatedly overdue, adjust your reminder system (e.g., set earlier alerts or use a more visible checklist)

If you notice recurring issues (e.g., frequent low oil), add a "watch list" section to your logbook to monitor potential problems

Security and preventive maintenance

Review and update the maintenance logbook at every oil change or at least every 3 months

Store digital backups of your logbook and receipts in a secure cloud service to prevent loss from fire or theft

Never skip critical services like timing belt replacement or brake fluid flush; mark these in red on your checklist and set multiple reminders

Inspect the logbook and folder for completeness before long road trips or before state inspections

Keep a spare pen and highlighter in the maintenance folder to ensure you can always update records on the go

Battery Inspection, Load Test and Terminal Cleaning

Materials and Tools

- Digital multimeter (auto-ranging, 0.1V accuracy, 0–20V DC range)
- Battery load tester (100–500 amp capacity, analog or digital, clamp or post type)
- Battery terminal cleaning brush (dual-ended, steel bristles)
- Baking soda (sodium bicarbonate, 1/4 cup)
- Distilled water (1 quart)
- Small plastic container (16 oz capacity)
- Clean shop towels (lint-free, 12x12 inch)
- Nitrile gloves (5–7 mil thickness)
- Safety glasses (ANSI Z87.1 rated)
- 1/2-inch box-end wrench or ratchet with 10mm socket (for terminal removal)
- Dielectric grease (tube, 1 oz, non-conductive)
- Wire brush (small, brass bristle)
- Battery post and terminal protector pads (felt, 2-pack)

- Battery hydrometer (for non-sealed batteries, 1.100–1.300 specific gravity range)
- Service manual (for battery specs and torque values)
- Disposable apron (polyethylene, for acid splash protection)

Step-by-step instructions

1. Park the vehicle on a flat, paved surface; turn off the ignition, remove the key, and engage the parking brake
2. Open the hood and locate the battery; verify the battery is cool to the touch before proceeding
3. Put on nitrile gloves, safety glasses, and a disposable apron to protect against acid and corrosion
4. Inspect the battery case for cracks, bulges, or leaks; if any are found, do not proceed—replace the battery immediately
5. Check the battery label for date code; if older than 5 years, plan for replacement regardless of test results
6. Examine battery terminals and cable ends for corrosion (white, green, or blue powder); note any loose or damaged clamps
7. Using a digital multimeter, set to DC volts; touch the red probe to the positive (+) terminal and black probe to the negative (–) terminal
8. Record the resting voltage; a healthy, fully charged battery should read 12.6–12.8V; 12.4V is 75% charged, 12.2V is 50%, below 12.0V is discharged
9. If the battery is not maintenance-free, carefully remove the vent caps and use a hydrometer to draw electrolyte from each cell; record specific gravity (normal: 1.265–1.299 at 77°F); replace caps securely
10. For load testing, connect the battery load tester clamps to the terminals (red to positive, black to negative); ensure a solid connection
11. Apply a load equal to half the battery's cold cranking amps (CCA) rating for 15 seconds; observe voltage drop
12. During the test, voltage should remain above 9.6V at 70°F; if it drops below, the battery is weak or failing
13. Remove the load tester and disconnect any accessories; do not attempt to load test a visibly damaged or leaking battery
14. To clean terminals, mix 1 tablespoon baking soda with 1 cup distilled water in a plastic container; stir until dissolved
15. Loosen and remove the negative (–) cable first using a 10mm wrench, then the positive (+) cable; set cables aside, avoiding contact with metal parts
16. Dip the terminal cleaning brush in the baking soda solution; scrub both battery posts and cable ends thoroughly to remove all corrosion
17. For stubborn deposits, use a small brass wire brush; avoid splashing solution onto paint or clothing
18. Rinse the cleaned areas with distilled water and dry with a clean shop towel
19. Reinstall the positive (+) cable first, then the negative (–); tighten to manufacturer's torque spec (typically 50–70 in-lbs)
20. Apply a thin layer of dielectric grease to each terminal and install felt protector pads if available
21. Close the hood, start the engine, and verify normal cranking speed

and no warning lights

Illustrations and diagrams

Diagram of battery terminal and cable layout with correct probe and tester placement
Cross-section of battery cell showing hydrometer use and specific gravity scale
Step-by-step illustration of terminal cleaning process with before/after corrosion detail
Chart of battery voltage vs. state of charge and load test pass/fail thresholds

Practical expert tips

Always remove the negative cable first and reconnect it last to prevent accidental short circuits
If corrosion is severe and extends under the insulation, replace the cable end or entire cable to prevent future starting issues
Use only distilled water for rinsing; tap water can introduce minerals that accelerate corrosion
Mark the battery installation date on the case with a permanent marker for easy future reference
If the battery repeatedly fails load tests but alternator output is normal, replace the battery—do not attempt to "revive" with repeated jump starts

Troubleshooting techniques

If the battery voltage is low but passes the load test, check for parasitic drain (current draw over 50mA with ignition off)
If the battery fails the load test but is less than 3 years old, check for loose or dirty terminals before replacing

If the engine cranks slowly but battery tests good, inspect starter and ground connections for high resistance
If corrosion returns quickly after cleaning, check for overcharging (alternator output above 14.7V) or leaking battery acid

Security and preventive maintenance

Inspect battery terminals and cables every 3 months or at every oil change for early signs of corrosion
Clean and protect terminals annually, even if no corrosion is visible, to ensure reliable starting
Replace batteries proactively every 4–5 years, especially in extreme climates, to avoid unexpected failure
Keep the battery top clean and dry; moisture and dirt can create conductive paths and accelerate self-discharge
Log all battery tests, cleanings, and replacements in your maintenance record for future reference

Serpentine and Timing Belt Inspection with Tensioner Check and Replacement

Materials and Tools

- Serpentine belt (EPDM, vehicle-specific length and rib count, e.g., 6PK1040 for many V6 engines)
- Timing belt kit (includes belt, tensioner, idler pulleys, water pump if required, all vehicle-specific)
- Belt tension gauge (mechanical or digital, 30–300 lbs range, 1-lb increments)
- 3/8-inch and 1/2-inch drive ratchets with metric socket set (8–19mm)
- Breaker bar (18–24 inch, for stubborn bolts)
- Torque wrench (5–100 ft-lbs, 1 ft-lb increments)
- Flat-blade screwdriver (6-inch shaft, 1/4-inch tip)
- Inspection mirror (2-inch diameter, telescoping handle)
- LED work light (1000 lumens, magnetic base)
- White paint marker (for alignment marks)
- Replacement tensioner (spring-loaded or hydraulic, vehicle-specific)
- Replacement idler pulleys (if worn, vehicle-specific)
- Service manual (OEM or reputable aftermarket, for torque specs and belt routing)
- Nitrile gloves (5–7 mil thickness)
- Shop towels (lint-free, 12x12 inch)
- Safety glasses (ANSI Z87.1 rated)
- Jack and jack stands (3-ton capacity, for engine support if required)
- Fender cover (to protect paint)
- Zip ties (8-inch, for holding components out of the way)
- Digital camera or smartphone (for reference photos)

Step-by-step instructions

1. Park the vehicle on a level surface, engage the parking brake, and disconnect the negative battery terminal using a 10mm wrench
2. Open the hood and install a fender cover to protect paint; position the LED work light for maximum visibility of the belt area
3. For serpentine belt inspection, locate the belt at the front of the engine; use the inspection mirror and light to examine the entire length, including hidden sections
4. Check for cracks across the ribs, missing chunks, fraying, glazing (shiny spots), or contamination (oil, coolant); replace if any of these are present or if the belt is over 60,000 miles old
5. Use the belt tension gauge to measure tension at the longest span between pulleys; compare to the manufacturer's spec (typically 90–160 lbs for serpentine belts); if tension is below spec, proceed to tensioner check
6. For tensioner inspection, locate the automatic tensioner (spring-loaded or hydraulic); with a 3/8-inch ratchet, rotate the tensioner through its full range—feel for smooth, even resistance and listen for grinding or squeaking
7. Observe the tensioner pulley for wobble, roughness, or play; spin by hand and check for noise or resistance—replace if any issues are found
8. If replacing the serpentine belt, use the ratchet or breaker bar to relieve tension by rotating the tensioner; slide the belt off the pulleys, noting the routing (take a photo or refer to the diagram)
9. Install the new belt, following the correct routing; ensure all ribs are fully seated in pulley grooves;

release the tensioner slowly to apply tension

10. Recheck belt tension with the gauge; adjust if manual tensioner is used, or verify automatic tensioner is functioning
11. For timing belt inspection, remove any necessary covers (typically plastic, secured with 10mm bolts); refer to the service manual for access steps—may require removal of engine mount or accessories
12. Rotate the crankshaft clockwise using a 1/2-inch ratchet and appropriate socket on the crank bolt; align timing marks on the crank and cam pulleys as per the manual
13. Inspect the timing belt for cracks, missing teeth, glazing, or oil contamination; check for excessive slack (should deflect no more than 1/4 inch at the longest span)
14. Inspect the timing belt tensioner and idler pulleys for leaks (hydraulic), roughness, or play; spin pulleys by hand and listen for noise
15. If replacement is needed, mark the current belt and pulleys with a white paint marker to preserve timing alignment
16. Loosen the tensioner bolt(s) and remove the old belt; do not rotate the cam or crank pulleys independently to avoid losing timing
17. Install the new timing belt, aligning all timing marks; install new tensioner and idler pulleys as provided in the kit
18. Apply tension as specified: for spring-loaded tensioners, release the pin; for manual, use the tension gauge and torque to spec (e.g., 33 ft-lbs)
19. Rotate the crankshaft two full turns by hand and recheck timing marks; verify belt tension and adjust if necessary
20. Reinstall all covers, engine mount, and accessories in reverse order; torque all bolts to manufacturer's specs
21. Reconnect the negative battery terminal, remove tools and fender cover, and start the engine; listen for abnormal noises and observe belt tracking for 2-3 minutes

Illustrations and diagrams

Diagram of serpentine belt routing with labeled pulleys and tensioner
Cross-section of timing belt system showing cam, crank, tensioner, and idler pulleys
Step-by-step illustration of tensioner removal and installation
Photo example of worn vs. new belt surfaces and common failure patterns

Practical expert tips

Always replace the tensioner and idler pulleys when installing a new timing belt, even if they appear good—failure of these components can destroy a new belt
Use a white paint marker to make alignment marks on the old belt and pulleys before removal; transfer marks to the new belt for foolproof timing
If the belt is contaminated with oil or coolant, address the source of the leak before installing a new belt to prevent premature failure
Take clear photos of belt routing and timing marks before disassembly for easy reference during reassembly
For vehicles with limited access, use zip ties to temporarily hold the new belt in place on the pulleys during

installation

Troubleshooting techniques

If the new belt squeals after installation, check for misalignment, improper tension, or a seized pulley
If the engine runs rough or won't start after timing belt replacement, recheck timing marks—one tooth off can cause major issues
If the tensioner does not maintain proper tension, verify correct installation and that the tensioner is the correct part number for your vehicle
If the belt walks off a pulley, inspect all pulleys for damage or misalignment and ensure the belt is fully seated in all grooves

Security and preventive maintenance

Inspect serpentine and timing belts every 12 months or 12,000 miles, whichever comes first
Replace serpentine belts every 60,000–90,000 miles and timing belts every 60,000–100,000 miles, per manufacturer recommendations
Log all inspections, tension checks, and replacements in your maintenance record, noting mileage and date
After any belt or tensioner replacement, recheck tension and condition after 500 miles to catch early issues
Store removed belts and tensioners for comparison until the new parts have proven reliable for at least 1,000 miles

Engine Air Filter and Cabin Filter Replacement with Intake and Ventilation Cleaning

Materials and Tools

- Engine air filter (OEM or high-quality aftermarket, vehicle-specific size and shape)
- Cabin air filter (HEPA or carbon-activated, vehicle-specific)
- Phillips and flathead screwdrivers (6-inch shaft, #2 tip)
- 1/4-inch drive ratchet with 8mm and 10mm sockets
- Torx bit set (T20–T30, for some airbox covers)
- Shop vacuum with crevice and brush attachments (5+ HP, HEPA filter recommended)
- Compressed air canister (minimum 100 psi, with straw nozzle)
- Clean microfiber towels (16x16 inch, lint-free)
- All-purpose automotive cleaner (non-residue, 16 oz spray bottle)
- Nitrile gloves (5–7 mil thickness)
- Safety glasses (ANSI Z87.1 rated)
- Small paintbrush (1-inch, natural bristle, for dusting vents)
- Service manual (for filter locations and access procedures)
- Replacement air intake duct seal (if original is cracked or missing)
- Cabin vent deodorizer spray

(automotive, non-oily, 8 oz)

Step-by-step instructions

1. Park the vehicle on a level surface, turn off the ignition, remove the key, and engage the parking brake
2. Open the hood and locate the engine air filter housing, typically a black plastic box near the front or side of the engine bay
3. Release the housing clips or remove screws/bolts using the appropriate screwdriver or socket; carefully lift the cover without forcing or bending attached hoses
4. Remove the old engine air filter, noting its orientation; inspect the filter for excessive dirt, oil, or debris —replace if any is present or if the filter is over 15,000 miles old
5. Use a shop vacuum with a crevice tool to thoroughly clean the inside of the airbox, removing all loose dirt, leaves, and insects; avoid damaging the air flow sensor if present
6. Inspect the air intake duct for cracks, loose connections, or missing seals; replace the duct seal if it is brittle or damaged to prevent unfiltered air entry
7. Use a compressed air canister to blow out any remaining dust from the airbox and intake duct, directing air away from the engine and electrical components
8. Wipe the airbox interior and cover with a clean microfiber towel lightly sprayed with all-purpose cleaner; allow to dry completely
9. Install the new engine air filter, ensuring the rubber gasket seats evenly around the perimeter and the pleats face the incoming air
10. Reinstall the airbox cover, securing all clips, screws, or bolts to the manufacturer's torque spec (typically 20–30 in-lbs); double-check for proper fit and seal
11. Move to the cabin air filter: locate the filter access panel, usually behind the glove box or under the dashboard on the passenger side (refer to the service manual for exact location)
12. Remove the glove box by releasing side stops or removing screws as needed; lower it fully to access the filter housing
13. Open the cabin filter housing by releasing tabs or removing screws; carefully slide out the old filter, noting airflow direction arrows
14. Inspect the old cabin filter for dirt, leaves, or mold; if heavily soiled or over 12,000 miles old, replace with a new filter of the same type (HEPA or carbon-activated)
15. Use a shop vacuum with a brush attachment to clean the filter housing and surrounding area, removing all dust and debris
16. Insert the new cabin filter, aligning airflow arrows with the direction indicated on the housing; ensure a snug, even fit with no gaps
17. Reinstall the filter cover and glove box, securing all fasteners and ensuring smooth operation
18. Clean the dashboard air vents by gently brushing with a 1-inch paintbrush to dislodge dust, then vacuum with a crevice tool
19. Spray a small amount of cabin vent deodorizer into the intake vents (usually at the base of the windshield) with the fan set to high and recirculation off; allow the system to run for 2–3 minutes to distribute the cleaner
20. Wipe all vent surfaces with a microfiber towel dampened with all-

purpose cleaner to remove any remaining residue

Illustrations and diagrams

Diagram of engine air filter housing with labeled clips, screws, and airflow direction
Cross-section of cabin air filter location behind glove box, showing filter orientation and airflow arrows
Step-by-step illustration of airbox cleaning and filter installation
Diagram of dashboard vent cleaning process with brush and vacuum attachments

Practical expert tips

Always check the service manual for filter type and replacement interval; some vehicles require special tools or have hidden fasteners
Mark the installation date and mileage on the filter frame with a permanent marker for easy future reference
If the air filter is found oily, inspect the PCV system for leaks or excessive blow-by
For allergy-sensitive drivers, choose a HEPA or carbon-activated cabin filter for maximum filtration of pollen and odors
Replace the air intake duct seal whenever it shows signs of cracking to prevent unfiltered air from bypassing the filter

Troubleshooting techniques

If engine performance drops or fuel economy worsens after filter replacement, check for airbox leaks, improper filter seating, or disconnected intake hoses
If cabin airflow is weak after filter replacement, verify the filter is installed in the correct direction and that no packaging material was left behind
If musty odors persist after cleaning, inspect the evaporator drain for clogs and consider using an HVAC system cleaner
If dashboard vents rattle or whistle, check for debris lodged in the vent vanes or loose vent assemblies

Security and preventive maintenance

Inspect engine and cabin air filters every 12,000–15,000 miles or at every oil change, whichever comes first
Clean air intake ducts and vent housings annually to prevent buildup of debris and allergens
Log all filter replacements and cleanings in your maintenance record, noting date and mileage
Use only filters that meet or exceed OEM specifications to ensure proper fit and filtration
Keep the area around the air intake (cowl and hood seals) free of leaves and debris to prevent clogging and water intrusion

4 PREVENTIVE MAINTENANCE PROJECTS

Monthly Preventive Maintenance Walkaround and Digital Log

THE CAR MAINTENANCE AND REPAIR BIBLE

Materials and Tools

- LED flashlight (1000 lumens, adjustable beam, rechargeable or with fresh AA batteries)
- Tire pressure gauge (digital, 0–100 psi, 0.5 psi increments)
- 12-inch steel ruler or digital tread depth gauge (0–1 inch, 1/32-inch increments)
- Clean microfiber towels (16x16 inch, lint-free)
- Nitrile gloves (5–7 mil thickness)
- Safety glasses (ANSI Z87.1 rated)
- Digital camera or smartphone (12MP or higher, with flash)
- OBD-II scanner (Bluetooth or handheld, compatible with vehicle year/make)
- Windshield washer fluid (1-gallon, all-season formula)
- Service manual (OEM or reputable aftermarket, for spec reference)
- Digital maintenance log app (e.g., Carfax Car Care, Drivvo, or spreadsheet on phone/tablet)
- Pen and notepad (for backup notes)
- Tire tread wear indicator card (optional, for quick visual check)
- Small flathead screwdriver (6-inch shaft, 1/4-inch tip, for battery terminal checks)
- Shop vacuum (5+ HP, for cleaning debris from engine bay and cowl area)

Step-by-step instructions

1. Park the vehicle on a level, well-lit surface; engage the parking brake and turn off the engine
2. Put on nitrile gloves and safety glasses for protection
3. Walk around the vehicle, starting at the driver's side front; use the LED flashlight to inspect all exterior lights (headlights, turn signals, brake lights, reverse lights, license plate lights) by activating each function and observing for dim, flickering, or non-working bulbs
4. Check windshield and windows for chips, cracks, or excessive pitting; note any damage in the digital log and photograph for reference
5. Inspect windshield wiper blades for cracks, splits, or missing rubber; gently lift each blade and run a finger along the edge—replace if rough or torn
6. Open the hood; use the flashlight to check for fluid leaks, frayed belts, cracked hoses, or loose connections; photograph any issues and log them
7. Check engine oil level and color using the dipstick; wipe, reinsert, and read—oil should be between min and max marks and amber to brown, not black or milky; log mileage and oil condition
8. Inspect coolant reservoir for proper level (between min and max lines) and color (should be clear, not rusty or oily); top off with correct coolant if needed and log the action
9. Check brake fluid reservoir for level and clarity; fluid should be between min and max, and light amber—note any drop or darkening in the log

10. Inspect power steering and transmission fluid (if accessible) for level and color per service manual; log findings

11. Examine battery terminals for corrosion (white or green buildup); gently wiggle cables to check for tightness; clean with a towel if needed and log any issues

12. Use the OBD-II scanner to check for stored or pending trouble codes; record any codes in the digital log and clear if appropriate

13. Inspect tires for visible damage, bulges, or embedded objects; use the digital tread depth gauge to measure tread at three points across each tire—replace if below 4/32 inch; log tread depth and tire condition

14. Use the tire pressure gauge to check each tire (including spare) when cold; inflate to manufacturer's spec (usually 32–36 psi, check door jamb sticker); log pressures and any adjustments

15. Check for uneven tire wear patterns (cupping, feathering, one-sided wear); photograph and log for future alignment or rotation needs

16. Open all doors, hood, and trunk; inspect weatherstripping for cracks or gaps; clean debris with a microfiber towel and log any damage

17. Check under the vehicle for fresh fluid spots or drips; note location, color, and approximate size in the log

18. Clean leaves and debris from the cowl area and engine bay with a shop vacuum to prevent water intrusion and clogging

19. Top off windshield washer fluid; test spray pattern and wiper operation; log refill

20. Review all findings and actions in the digital maintenance log app, attaching photos and notes for each item; set reminders for follow-up or repairs as needed

Illustrations and diagrams

Diagram of walkaround inspection path with numbered checkpoints (lights, glass, tires, undercarriage, engine bay)

Cross-section of tire showing tread depth measurement points and wear patterns

Illustration of fluid reservoir locations under the hood with min/max markings

Step-by-step photo sequence of digital log entry on a smartphone app

Practical expert tips

Always perform the walkaround at the same time each month (e.g., first Saturday) to build a habit and catch issues early

Use your phone's voice memo feature to quickly record findings if your hands are dirty, then transcribe into the log later

Photograph any new damage or leaks immediately—visual records help track progression and support warranty or insurance claims

If you find a low tire, check for nails or punctures before inflating; mark the spot with chalk for easy repair identification

Keep a spare set of bulbs and fuses in your glove box for quick light replacements

Troubleshooting techniques

If a light is out but the bulb looks good, check the fuse box (refer to manual for location and fuse rating) and replace blown fuses with the correct amperage

If you find repeated low tire pressure, inspect the valve stem for leaks using soapy water—bubbles indicate a slow leak

If the OBD-II scanner shows a code but no warning light, research the code online or in the manual; some codes are pending and may resolve after a few drive cycles

If you notice fluid under the car, use a white towel to dab the spot—engine oil is brown/black, coolant is usually green/orange/pink, transmission fluid is red, brake fluid is clear to amber

Security and preventive maintenance

Schedule a monthly reminder on your phone or calendar for the walkaround and log update

Back up your digital maintenance log to cloud storage or email a copy to yourself after each entry

Review previous months' logs to spot recurring issues or trends (e.g., slow oil loss, repeated tire wear)

Keep all receipts and service records attached to your digital log for warranty and resale value

Share your log with your mechanic during professional service visits to provide a complete maintenance history

Cooling System Hose, Clamp and Radiator Care with Pressure Test

Materials and Tools

- Radiator pressure tester kit (0–30 psi gauge, multiple cap adapters, hand pump)
- Replacement radiator hoses (upper and lower, EPDM rubber, vehicle-specific diameter and length)
- Stainless steel worm gear hose clamps (1/2–1-1/4 inch for most cars, 5/16-inch hex head)
- Coolant (50/50 premix, ethylene glycol-based, compatible with vehicle spec, minimum 2 gallons)
- Distilled water (1 gallon, for flushing and topping off)
- Large drain pan (minimum 3-gallon capacity, chemical-resistant plastic)
- Long-handle flathead screwdriver (8-inch shaft, 1/4-inch tip)
- 1/4-inch drive ratchet with 8mm and 10mm sockets
- Utility knife with fresh blade (for hose removal)
- Clean shop rags (lint-free, 12x12 inch)
- Nitrile gloves (7 mil thickness)
- Safety glasses (ANSI Z87.1 rated)
- LED inspection mirror (2-inch diameter, telescoping handle)
- Digital thermometer (0–250°F range, probe style)
- Torque wrench (inch-pound scale, 30–80 in-lbs for clamp tightening)

- Service manual (for torque specs, hose routing, and coolant type)
- Funnel with integrated mesh screen (for filling coolant)
- Garden hose with spray nozzle (for flushing, if needed)
- Zip ties (8-inch, for securing loose wiring or hoses)

Step-by-step instructions

1. Park the vehicle on a level surface, allow the engine to cool for at least 2 hours, and engage the parking brake
2. Put on nitrile gloves and safety glasses to protect against hot coolant and sharp edges
3. Place a 3-gallon drain pan under the radiator drain plug or lower hose connection
4. Open the radiator cap slowly to release any residual pressure; use a shop rag to shield your hand in case of steam
5. Open the radiator drain plug (usually 19mm plastic or brass) or loosen the lower radiator hose clamp with a flathead screwdriver; allow coolant to drain completely
6. Inspect drained coolant for rust, oil, or debris; note any contamination for further troubleshooting
7. Use a flashlight and inspection mirror to examine all radiator hoses (upper, lower, heater hoses) for cracks, bulges, soft spots, or oil contamination; squeeze each hose—replace if spongy or excessively hard
8. Check all hose clamps for corrosion, looseness, or stripped threads; replace with new stainless steel clamps if any are damaged or rusted
9. Remove old hoses by loosening clamps fully and twisting the hose gently; if stuck, carefully slit the hose lengthwise with a utility knife and peel off—avoid scratching the metal necks
10. Clean all hose necks and radiator fittings with a shop rag to remove old residue and corrosion
11. Install new hoses, ensuring they are fully seated on the necks (at least 1 inch overlap); orient clamps 1/4 inch from the hose end and position the screw for easy future access
12. Tighten hose clamps evenly to 30–40 in-lbs with a torque wrench; do not overtighten, as this can cut into the hose
13. Inspect the radiator for bent fins, leaks, or white crusty deposits (dried coolant); use a garden hose to gently flush debris from the fins, spraying from the engine side out
14. Check the radiator cap for a clean, undamaged rubber seal and spring tension; replace if the seal is cracked or the cap is rated below the vehicle's specified pressure (usually 13–16 psi)
15. Attach the radiator pressure tester to the filler neck; pump to the cap's rated pressure (e.g., 15 psi) and observe the gauge for 2 minutes—pressure should not drop more than 1 psi
16. If pressure drops, inspect all hose connections, radiator seams, and water pump for leaks; tighten clamps or replace faulty components as needed
17. Remove the tester, reinstall the radiator cap, and close the drain plug securely
18. Fill the radiator with 50/50 premix coolant using a funnel with mesh screen to catch debris; fill until coolant reaches the neck, then fill

the overflow reservoir to the "MAX" line

19. Start the engine and run at idle with the heater set to maximum; monitor temperature with a digital thermometer at the upper hose—ensure it reaches 180–210°F and check for leaks as the system pressurizes

20. Squeeze the upper radiator hose with a gloved hand to confirm it is hot and pressurized (thermostat open); top off coolant as needed

21. After engine cools, recheck coolant level and inspect all hose connections for seepage; retighten clamps if necessary

Illustrations and diagrams

Diagram of cooling system layout showing upper/lower radiator hoses, heater hoses, clamps, and radiator cap
Cross-section of hose clamp installation with correct positioning and torque
Step-by-step illustration of pressure tester setup and leak check
Diagram of radiator fin cleaning with spray direction and debris removal

Practical expert tips

Always use new clamps when replacing hoses—old clamps can lose tension and cause leaks
Mark the installation date and mileage on each new hose with a paint marker for future reference
If a hose is oily, check for engine oil leaks above the hose—oil degrades rubber rapidly
Use only distilled water for mixing or topping off coolant to prevent mineral buildup
When flushing the radiator, run the heater to ensure the heater core is cleaned as well

Troubleshooting techniques

If pressure drops rapidly during the test, check for coolant dripping under the car or hissing at hose ends
If the radiator cap fails to hold pressure, replace it with a cap matching the OEM pressure rating
If hoses repeatedly become soft or swollen, suspect a head gasket leak contaminating the coolant
If the engine overheats after hose replacement, check for trapped air—bleed the system per the service manual

Security and preventive maintenance

Inspect all cooling system hoses and clamps every 12 months or 12,000 miles for early signs of wear
Replace radiator hoses every 5 years or 60,000 miles, even if they appear intact
Log all hose, clamp, and coolant replacements in your maintenance record with date and mileage
Keep a spare radiator cap and short length of hose in your emergency kit for roadside repairs
Never open the radiator cap when the engine is hot—wait until fully cooled to avoid burns

Brake System Preventive Service: Pad Measurement, Caliper Lubrication and Rotor Dressing

THE CAR MAINTENANCE AND REPAIR BIBLE

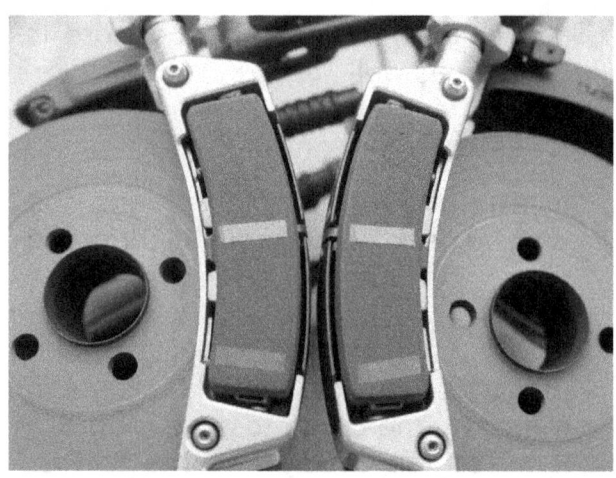

Materials and Tools

- Digital brake pad thickness gauge (0–20 mm range, 0.01 mm increments)
- 3/8-inch drive torque wrench (10–80 ft-lbs range, ±4% accuracy)
- 1/2-inch drive breaker bar (18-inch length)
- 17 mm and 19 mm 6-point sockets (for most lug nuts and caliper bolts)
- Flathead screwdriver (6-inch shaft, 1/4-inch tip)
- Synthetic high-temperature brake caliper grease (rated to 500°F+)
- 3M brake cleaner spray (non-chlorinated, 14 oz can)
- 320-grit and 600-grit sandpaper sheets (9x11 inch, aluminum oxide)
- Clean shop rags (lint-free, 12x12 inch)
- Nitrile gloves (7 mil thickness)
- Safety glasses (ANSI Z87.1 rated)
- Floor jack (2-ton minimum, with rubber pad)
- Jack stands (2-ton minimum, ANSI certified)
- Wheel chocks (rubber, 8-inch length)
- Wire brush (stainless steel, 8-inch handle)
- Bungee cord (24-inch, for caliper support)
- Service manual (for torque specs and pad minimum thickness)
- Digital caliper (0–6 inch, for rotor thickness measurement)
- Masking tape (1-inch wide, for marking pad orientation)
- Small paintbrush (1-inch, for applying grease)
- Shop vacuum (5+ HP, for dust removal)

Step-by-step instructions

1. Park the vehicle on a level concrete surface; engage the parking brake and place wheel chocks behind the rear tires
2. Loosen lug nuts on the front wheels 1/2 turn with the breaker bar and correct socket before lifting the vehicle
3. Position the floor jack under the manufacturer's recommended lift point; raise the vehicle until the tire is 2 inches off the ground
4. Place jack stands under the frame or pinch welds; lower the vehicle onto the stands and confirm stability by gently rocking the car
5. Remove the lug nuts and wheel; set the wheel flat under the car as an extra safety measure
6. Use the digital brake pad thickness gauge to measure the outer and inner pad thickness at the thinnest point; record values in millimeters and compare to the service manual's minimum (typically 3 mm for replacement)
7. Mark the orientation of each pad with masking tape to ensure correct reinstallation
8. Inspect the rotor surface for scoring, grooves, or blue discoloration; use the digital caliper to measure rotor thickness at four points around the edge—replace if below minimum spec (usually 1.0–

1.2 inches for most cars)
9. Remove the caliper bolts with the 17 mm or 19 mm socket; support the caliper with a bungee cord from the suspension to prevent hose strain
10. Slide out the brake pads; note any uneven wear or glazing
11. Clean the caliper bracket and pad slides with a wire brush and brake cleaner; wipe dry with a shop rag
12. Apply a thin, even layer of synthetic high-temp brake caliper grease to the pad backing plates, caliper slide pins, and contact points—avoid getting grease on pad friction surfaces or rotors
13. Remove the rotor if accessible; use 320-grit sandpaper to dress the rotor face in a circular motion, removing glaze and light rust—follow with 600-grit for a smooth finish; vacuum dust and wipe with brake cleaner
14. Reinstall the rotor and pads in their original orientation; torque caliper bolts to the manufacturer's spec (typically 25–35 ft-lbs for most cars) using the torque wrench
15. Reinstall the wheel; hand-tighten lug nuts in a star pattern
16. Lower the vehicle off the jack stands; torque lug nuts to spec (usually 80–100 ft-lbs) with the torque wrench
17. Pump the brake pedal 5–7 times to seat the pads before driving
18. Repeat the process for the opposite side

Illustrations and diagrams

Diagram of brake assembly with labeled pad, caliper, rotor, and slide pin locations
Step-by-step illustration of pad thickness measurement with digital gauge
Cross-section of caliper showing correct grease application points
Rotor dressing technique with sandpaper motion arrows

Practical expert tips

Always measure both inner and outer pads—uneven wear may indicate a sticking caliper or slide pin
Use a shop vacuum to remove all brake dust before working; airborne dust can be harmful if inhaled
Mark pad orientation and caliper bolt locations with masking tape to avoid mix-ups during reassembly
If the rotor has deep grooves or is below minimum thickness, replace rather than dress it
Apply only a pea-sized amount of grease to slide pins—excess can attract dirt and cause binding

Troubleshooting techniques

If pads wear unevenly (inner thinner than outer), inspect and clean or replace caliper slide pins
If the caliper is difficult to retract, check for seized pistons or contaminated brake fluid
If you hear squealing after service, check for missing anti-rattle clips or grease on pad edges
If the pedal feels soft after reassembly, check for loose caliper bolts or air in the brake lines

Security and preventive maintenance

Inspect pad thickness and rotor condition every 6 months or 6,000 miles, whichever comes first
Lubricate caliper slide pins and pad

contact points at every pad change or annually
Log pad and rotor measurements, service dates, and any parts replaced in your maintenance record
Replace pads before reaching the minimum thickness to prevent rotor damage and ensure safe braking
Store a spare set of caliper bolts and a tube of high-temp grease in your garage for future service

Electrical System Preventive Check: Corrosion Control, Grounding and Connector Sealing

Materials and Tools

- Digital multimeter (auto-ranging, 0.1 mV–600 V DC/AC, continuity buzzer)
- Dielectric grease (silicone-based, 3 oz tube, -40°F to 400°F rated)
- Electrical contact cleaner spray (non-residue, 11 oz can)
- Nylon bristle brush (6-inch handle, for connector cleaning)
- 1/4-inch drive ratchet with 8 mm and 10 mm sockets
- Wire brush (stainless steel, 8-inch handle, for ground points)
- 220-grit emery cloth (1-inch wide, for terminal cleaning)
- Heat shrink tubing (3/16-inch and 1/4-inch diameter, adhesive-lined)
- Heat gun (1200W, variable temp, 600°F max)
- Nitrile gloves (7 mil thickness)
- Safety glasses (ANSI Z87.1 rated)
- Shop rags (lint-free, 12x12 inch)
- Zip ties (8-inch, UV-resistant)
- Service manual (for ground point and connector locations)
- Torque wrench (inch-pound scale, 30–80 in-lbs for ground bolts)
- Small flathead screwdriver (1/8-inch tip, for connector release tabs)
- Replacement ring terminals (copper, 10–12 AWG, tin-plated)
- Electrical tape (PVC, 3/4-inch wide, UL listed)

Step-by-step instructions

1. Park the vehicle on a level surface, turn off the ignition, and disconnect the negative battery terminal using a 10 mm socket to prevent accidental shorts
2. Consult the service manual to identify all major ground points (engine block, chassis, battery, fuse box) and critical electrical connectors (ECU, sensors, lighting harnesses)
3. Inspect visible wiring harnesses for cracked insulation, exposed copper, or signs of rodent damage; secure any loose harnesses with zip ties
4. Locate each ground point; remove the ground bolt with the correct socket, and detach the ring terminal from the chassis or engine block
5. Clean the ring terminal and mating surface with a wire brush and 220-grit emery cloth until shiny bare metal is exposed; wipe away debris with a shop rag

6. Spray both surfaces with electrical contact cleaner and allow to dry for 1 minute
7. Apply a thin, even layer of dielectric grease to the cleaned ring terminal and the chassis/engine contact area to prevent future corrosion
8. Reinstall the ground terminal and torque the bolt to the manufacturer's spec (typically 40–60 in-lbs); do not overtighten to avoid stripping threads
9. For connectors, release the locking tab with a small flathead screwdriver and gently separate the halves; inspect for green/white corrosion, bent pins, or moisture
10. Clean corroded pins with a nylon brush and contact cleaner; if corrosion is severe, replace the connector or affected pins using new terminals
11. Apply a small amount of dielectric grease to the male pins and inside the connector shell; avoid overfilling, which can impede connection
12. Reconnect the connector until the locking tab clicks; wrap exposed connectors with heat shrink tubing, shrinking it with a heat gun for a watertight seal
13. For any spliced or repaired wires, slide adhesive-lined heat shrink tubing over the joint and shrink until adhesive flows, ensuring a moisture barrier
14. Reconnect the negative battery terminal and torque to 40–50 in-lbs; start the vehicle and use a digital multimeter to check voltage drop across each ground point (should be less than 0.1 V with engine running)
15. Log all cleaned, greased, or replaced grounds and connectors in your maintenance record with date and mileage

Illustrations and diagrams

Diagram of vehicle electrical system showing main ground points and critical connectors
Cross-section of ground terminal cleaning and dielectric grease application
Step-by-step illustration of connector disassembly, cleaning, greasing, and sealing with heat shrink tubing
Multimeter setup for voltage drop testing at ground points

Practical expert tips

Always disconnect the battery before working on electrical connectors to prevent accidental shorts or airbag deployment
Use only adhesive-lined heat shrink tubing for outdoor or underhood connectors—standard tubing does not seal out moisture
Mark cleaned ground points with a paint pen for easy future identification
If a connector is difficult to separate, never force it—use a small amount of contact cleaner to loosen and gently wiggle free
Store a tube of dielectric grease and a small brush in your glove box for emergency roadside repairs

Troubleshooting techniques

If you find repeated corrosion at the same ground point, check for water leaks or missing splash shields above the area
If a connector shows intermittent function after cleaning, inspect for loose or bent pins and replace as needed

If voltage drop across a ground exceeds 0.1 V, re-clean the terminal and check for broken wires or hidden corrosion under insulation

If you notice electrical gremlins (flickering lights, erratic sensors), systematically check and clean all grounds and connectors in the affected circuit

Security and preventive maintenance

Inspect all major ground points and critical connectors every 12 months or 12,000 miles, whichever comes first

Apply dielectric grease to all new or serviced connectors and ground points to prevent moisture intrusion

Replace any corroded or damaged terminals immediately to avoid electrical fires or system failures

Log all preventive electrical maintenance in your service record, noting date, mileage, and specific locations serviced

Keep a small kit with contact cleaner, dielectric grease, and heat shrink tubing in your garage for regular upkeep

CHAPTER 13: FOUR INTERIOR & EXTERIOR CARE PROJECTS

Leather Seat Cleaning, Conditioning, and Small Tear Repair

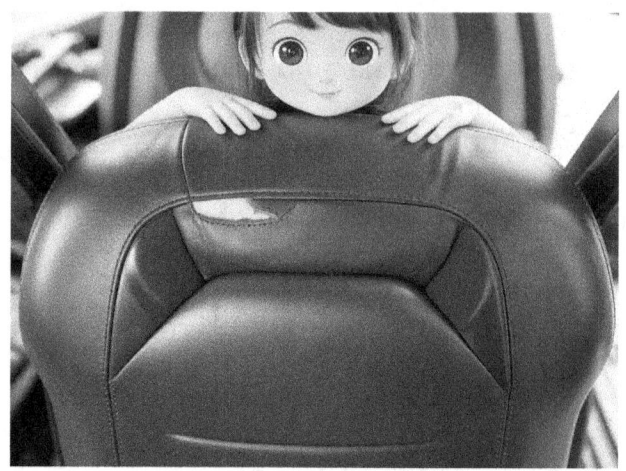

Materials and Tools

- pH-balanced leather cleaner (spray or gel, 16 oz bottle, pH 6–7)
- Soft-bristle leather cleaning brush (horsehair, 6-inch handle)
- Microfiber towels (16x16 inch, 300+ GSM, lint-free, 4 pieces)
- Leather conditioner (lanolin-based, 8 oz jar, non-greasy finish)
- Leather repair kit (includes color-matched filler, adhesive, grain paper, spatula, 1 oz each)
- Isopropyl alcohol (70%, 4 oz bottle)
- Cotton swabs (6-inch, wooden handle)
- Fine-grit sandpaper (600-grit, 3x5 inch sheet)
- Nitrile gloves (7 mil thickness)
- Small heat gun (1200W, variable temp, 600°F max)
- Masking tape (1-inch wide, for repair area)
- Color-matched leather dye (1 oz bottle, water-based)
- Small foam applicator pad (2-inch diameter)
- Service manual (for seat removal, if needed)

Step-by-step instructions

1. Vacuum the seat surface thoroughly using a soft brush

attachment to remove all loose dirt and debris, paying special attention to seams and crevices
2. Spray pH-balanced leather cleaner directly onto a soft-bristle brush; gently scrub the leather in small circular motions, working one 12x12 inch section at a time
3. Wipe away loosened dirt and excess cleaner immediately with a clean microfiber towel; repeat until the entire seat is clean and residue-free
4. For stubborn stains, apply a small amount of cleaner to a microfiber towel and rub the area with moderate pressure; avoid soaking the leather
5. Allow the seat to air dry for 10 minutes before proceeding
6. Inspect for small tears or cracks (up to 1 inch long); mark the area with masking tape to isolate the repair zone
7. Clean the repair area with a cotton swab dipped in isopropyl alcohol to remove oils and ensure proper adhesion; let dry for 2 minutes
8. Lightly sand the edges of the tear with 600-grit sandpaper to feather and smooth the surface; wipe away dust with a microfiber towel
9. Using the leather repair kit, apply a thin layer of adhesive under the tear with the spatula, pressing the edges together; hold for 1 minute until tacky
10. Fill the tear with color-matched filler in thin layers, smoothing each layer with the spatula; allow each layer to dry for 5 minutes or use a heat gun on low for 30 seconds to speed curing
11. Once the filler is level with the surrounding leather, press the included grain paper over the repair and apply gentle heat with the heat gun for 30 seconds to imprint texture
12. Remove the grain paper and inspect the repair; lightly sand if needed for a seamless finish
13. Dab color-matched leather dye onto the repaired area with a foam applicator pad, blending outward to match the original color; allow to dry for 10 minutes, repeating as needed for full coverage
14. Once the repair is fully dry, apply a small amount of leather conditioner to a clean microfiber towel and massage into the entire seat in overlapping circles
15. Let the conditioner absorb for 15 minutes, then buff the seat with a dry microfiber towel to remove excess and restore a natural sheen

Illustrations and diagrams

Diagram of seat cross-section showing tear location and repair layering
Step-by-step illustration of cleaning, adhesive application, filler layering, and grain paper use
Color blending chart for matching leather dye to seat color
Diagram of correct circular cleaning and conditioning motion

Practical expert tips

Always test cleaner and dye on a hidden area to check for colorfastness before full application
Use minimal water during cleaning—excess moisture can cause leather to stiffen or crack
For best results, perform repairs in a climate-controlled garage (60–75°F, low humidity)

Store leather conditioner in a cool, dark place to prevent spoilage and maintain effectiveness
If the tear is larger than 1 inch or in a high-stress area (seat edge, bolster), consult a professional upholsterer for structural repair

Troubleshooting techniques

If the filler shrinks or cracks after drying, apply additional thin layers and cure with heat until flush
If the repaired area feels sticky after dyeing, allow more drying time or use a heat gun on low for 30 seconds
If color mismatch occurs, mix small amounts of different dyes to achieve a closer match before final application
If the seat feels stiff after conditioning, apply a second light coat of conditioner and buff thoroughly

Security and preventive maintenance

Clean and condition leather seats every 3 months or 3,000 miles, whichever comes first
Address small tears or cracks immediately to prevent spreading and moisture intrusion
Avoid parking in direct sunlight for extended periods; use sunshades to reduce UV damage
Log all cleaning, conditioning, and repairs in your maintenance record with date and products used
Keep a small leather care kit in your trunk for quick touch-ups and emergency repairs

Fabric Upholstery Stain Removal and Odor Neutralization

Materials and Tools

- Enzyme-based upholstery cleaner (spray, 22 oz bottle, safe for automotive fabrics)
- Oxygenated stain remover powder (sodium percarbonate, 1 lb tub, color-safe)
- Distilled water (1 gallon jug)
- Spray bottle (32 oz, adjustable nozzle)
- Soft-bristle upholstery brush (nylon, 6-inch handle)
- White microfiber towels (16x16 inch, 300+ GSM, lint-free, 6 pieces)
- Wet/dry vacuum (4+ gallon, with upholstery nozzle)
- Baking soda (sodium bicarbonate, 16 oz box)
- Small plastic scoop (2 oz capacity)
- Nitrile gloves (7 mil thickness)
- UV flashlight (365 nm, for stain detection)
- Service manual (for seat removal, if needed)
- Portable fan (10-inch, 3-speed, for drying)
- Odor-neutralizing spray (chlorine dioxide-based, 16 oz bottle, non-

masking)

Step-by-step instructions

1. Park the vehicle in a well-ventilated area with all doors open; position a portable fan to direct airflow through the cabin
2. Inspect upholstery under natural light and with a UV flashlight to identify all stains and soiled areas; mark with small pieces of masking tape if needed
3. Vacuum the entire seat or carpeted area thoroughly using the upholstery nozzle, making multiple slow passes to remove loose dirt and debris
4. For fresh liquid stains, blot immediately with a clean, dry microfiber towel, applying firm downward pressure—do not rub, as this spreads the stain
5. Mix oxygenated stain remover: dissolve 1 scoop (2 oz) in 16 oz of warm distilled water in a spray bottle; shake until fully dissolved
6. Spray the stained area lightly with the solution, holding the nozzle 6 inches from the fabric; avoid oversaturating to prevent mold growth
7. Allow the solution to dwell for 10 minutes to activate stain-lifting action; keep the area damp but not soaked
8. Gently agitate the stain with a soft-bristle upholstery brush using small circular motions, working from the outside of the stain toward the center
9. Blot the area with a clean microfiber towel, pressing firmly to lift dissolved stain and excess moisture; repeat spraying, brushing, and blotting as needed until the stain is no longer visible
10. For protein-based stains (food, sweat, pet accidents), spray enzyme-based upholstery cleaner directly onto the affected area and let sit for 15 minutes to break down organic material
11. Blot and brush as above, then vacuum the area with the wet/dry vacuum to extract remaining moisture and cleaner residue
12. Sprinkle a thin, even layer of baking soda (about 1/4 cup per seat or 1 cup per carpeted footwell) over the cleaned area to absorb residual odors; let sit for at least 2 hours, or overnight for strong odors
13. Vacuum up all baking soda thoroughly, making multiple passes to ensure no powder remains in seams or crevices
14. If odors persist, lightly mist the area with a chlorine dioxide-based odor-neutralizing spray, holding the bottle 12 inches from the fabric; allow to air dry completely with fan assistance
15. Inspect the area for any remaining stains or odors; repeat the process as needed for stubborn spots
16. Log the cleaning date, products used, and any persistent issues in your maintenance record

Illustrations and diagrams

Diagram of seat cross-section showing stain penetration and cleaning action
Step-by-step illustration of blotting, spraying, brushing, and vacuuming techniques
UV flashlight detection of hidden stains on fabric
Diagram of proper baking soda application and vacuum removal

Practical expert tips

Always test cleaners and stain removers on a hidden section of upholstery to check for colorfastness before full application

Use only distilled water for mixing solutions to prevent mineral deposits and water spots on fabric

For deep-set or old stains, repeat the cleaning cycle up to three times, allowing full drying between applications

Avoid using colored towels or sponges, as dyes may transfer to upholstery during cleaning

If possible, remove seat cushions or floor mats for cleaning outside the vehicle to speed drying and improve access

Troubleshooting techniques

If a stain reappears after drying, it may have wicked up from deeper layers; repeat the cleaning process, focusing on slow, thorough extraction with the wet/dry vacuum

For persistent odors after cleaning, check for hidden sources under seats or carpet padding and treat those areas directly

If fabric feels stiff after cleaning, lightly mist with distilled water and brush with a soft-bristle brush to restore texture

If water marks appear, blend the edges by lightly dampening the surrounding area and blotting outward with a clean towel

Security and preventive maintenance

Clean fabric upholstery every 6 months or 6,000 miles, whichever comes first, to prevent buildup of stains and odors

Address spills and stains immediately to prevent permanent setting and bacterial growth

Use seat covers or floor mats in high-traffic areas to minimize direct soiling

Store a small emergency kit with enzyme cleaner, microfiber towels, and baking soda in your trunk for quick response to spills

Log all upholstery cleaning and odor treatments in your maintenance record, noting date, products, and any recurring issues

Interior Plastic and Vinyl Restoration with UV Protectant

Materials and Tools

- pH-neutral interior cleaner (spray, 16 oz bottle, safe for plastic and vinyl)
- Soft-bristle detailing brush (synthetic, 1-inch diameter, 6-inch handle)
- Microfiber towels (16x16 inch, 350+ GSM, lint-free, 4 pieces)
- Plastic and vinyl restorer (silicone-free, water-based, 8 oz bottle)
- UV protectant spray (SPF 50+, non-

greasy, 12 oz bottle)
- Foam applicator pads (3-inch diameter, closed-cell, 2 pieces)
- Detailing swabs (foam-tipped, 6-inch, for vents and seams)
- Isopropyl alcohol (70%, 4 oz bottle)
- Nitrile gloves (7 mil thickness)
- Masking tape (1-inch wide, for isolating trim)
- Service manual (for trim removal, if needed)

Step-by-step instructions

1. Park the vehicle in a shaded, well-ventilated area with all doors open to prevent rapid drying and ensure proper ventilation
2. Inspect all interior plastic and vinyl surfaces (dashboard, door panels, center console, trim) for fading, scratches, and embedded dirt; use a flashlight to check seams and textured areas
3. Use masking tape to protect adjacent fabric, leather, or glass surfaces from accidental contact with cleaners or restorers
4. Spray pH-neutral interior cleaner directly onto a soft-bristle detailing brush; gently agitate the surface in small circular motions, focusing on textured and high-touch areas
5. Wipe away loosened dirt and cleaner immediately with a clean microfiber towel; repeat until all surfaces are residue-free
6. For stubborn grime in seams, vents, or tight corners, use foam-tipped detailing swabs lightly moistened with cleaner; avoid oversaturating to prevent liquid seepage behind panels
7. Allow surfaces to air dry for 10 minutes; inspect for any remaining stains or discoloration
8. For faded or scratched areas, dampen a microfiber towel with isopropyl alcohol and gently wipe the affected zone to remove oils and prepare for restoration; let dry for 2 minutes
9. Apply a small amount (quarter-sized) of plastic and vinyl restorer to a foam applicator pad; work the product into the surface using overlapping strokes, applying moderate pressure for even coverage
10. Allow the restorer to penetrate for 5 minutes; buff off excess with a clean microfiber towel to prevent streaking or tackiness
11. Once the surface is dry and uniform in appearance, spray UV protectant evenly from 8 inches away, holding the bottle perpendicular to the surface; use 1-2 sprays per square foot for full coverage
12. Spread the protectant with a fresh foam applicator pad, ensuring all areas—including edges and seams—are coated; avoid pooling or oversaturation
13. Let the protectant cure for 15 minutes before touching or reinstalling any removed trim pieces
14. Remove masking tape carefully and inspect all surfaces for uniform sheen and color
15. Log the restoration date, products used, and any persistent issues in your maintenance record

Illustrations and diagrams

Diagram of dashboard cross-section showing layers of plastic/vinyl and UV penetration
Step-by-step illustration of cleaning, restoring, and protectant application on a door panel
Diagram of masking tape placement

to protect adjacent materials
Illustration of foam applicator pad technique for even product distribution

Practical expert tips

Always test restorer and protectant on a hidden area to check for color change or surface reaction before full application
Use separate applicator pads for restorer and protectant to prevent product cross-contamination
For heavily faded or chalky surfaces, apply two thin coats of restorer, allowing full drying between applications
Store all products in a cool, dry place and shake bottles well before use to ensure even distribution of active ingredients
Avoid using oil-based or greasy products, as they can attract dust and cause long-term discoloration

Troubleshooting techniques

If streaks or shiny patches appear after application, buff the area with a dry microfiber towel and reapply a thin layer of restorer or protectant as needed
For persistent fading, repeat the restoration process up to three times, allowing full drying between coats
If residue remains in textured surfaces, use a soft-bristle brush dampened with isopropyl alcohol to gently lift and remove buildup
If protectant leaves a sticky finish, reduce application amount and increase buffing time to achieve a dry, natural feel

Security and preventive maintenance

Reapply UV protectant every 3 months or 3,000 miles, especially in sunny climates or if the vehicle is parked outdoors frequently
Clean interior plastic and vinyl surfaces monthly to prevent buildup of dust, oils, and contaminants that accelerate fading
Use windshield sunshades and park in shaded areas whenever possible to minimize UV exposure
Inspect for early signs of cracking or discoloration during routine cleaning and address immediately to prevent permanent damage
Keep a small kit with cleaner, microfiber towel, and protectant in your glove box for quick touch-ups and emergency spills

Exterior Paint Scratch Touch-Up, Clear Coat Blending, and Polishing

Materials and Tools

- Automotive touch-up paint (OEM color-matched, 0.5 oz bottle with brush applicator)
- Clear coat touch-up (0.5 oz bottle,

compatible with base paint)
- 2000-grit wet/dry sandpaper (3 sheets, 9x3.6 inch)
- 3000-grit wet/dry sandpaper (2 sheets, 9x3.6 inch)
- Sanding block (2.5x4 inch, flexible foam)
- Isopropyl alcohol (70%, 8 oz bottle)
- Microfiber towels (16x16 inch, 350+ GSM, lint-free, 4 pieces)
- Masking tape (1-inch wide, automotive grade)
- Plastic sheeting (2x2 ft, for masking)
- Fine-tip paint brush (synthetic, 1/8 inch width)
- Toothpicks (wooden, for precision application)
- Polishing compound (non-abrasive, 8 oz bottle)
- Dual-action (DA) polisher (5-inch pad, variable speed, 2500–6500 OPM)
- Foam polishing pads (5-inch, medium and finishing grade, 2 each)
- Paint prep solution (wax and grease remover, 12 oz spray)
- Nitrile gloves (7 mil thickness)
- UV flashlight (365 nm, for clear coat inspection)
- Service manual (for paint code reference)

Step-by-step instructions

1. Park the vehicle in a dust-free, shaded area with ambient temperature between 60–80°F; avoid direct sunlight to prevent premature drying of paint and clear coat
2. Clean the scratched area thoroughly with paint prep solution and a microfiber towel, removing all wax, grease, and contaminants; allow to air dry for 5 minutes
3. Use masking tape and plastic sheeting to isolate a 2-inch perimeter around the scratch, protecting adjacent panels and trim from accidental paint or compound contact
4. Inspect the scratch depth: if the scratch catches a fingernail, it has penetrated the clear coat and may require touch-up paint; if not, proceed directly to polishing
5. For scratches through the clear coat, lightly sand the area with 2000-grit wet/dry sandpaper wrapped around a sanding block; lubricate with clean water and use gentle, even strokes along the direction of the scratch for 10–15 passes, checking progress frequently
6. Wipe the area with a clean microfiber towel and inspect under a UV flashlight to confirm the scratch is feathered and edges are smooth; repeat sanding with 3000-grit for 10 passes to refine the surface
7. Clean the sanded area with isopropyl alcohol and allow to dry completely
8. Shake the touch-up paint bottle for 60 seconds; use a fine-tip brush or toothpick to apply a thin layer of paint directly into the scratch, avoiding overlap onto undamaged paint; allow to dry for 30 minutes
9. Apply a second coat if needed for full color coverage, waiting 30 minutes between coats; do not overfill the scratch
10. Once the color coat is fully dry (minimum 2 hours), apply a thin layer of clear coat using a clean fine-tip brush, extending just beyond the edges of the touch-up paint; allow to dry for 1 hour
11. Apply a second clear coat layer if necessary for a level finish, waiting 1 hour between coats

12. After 24 hours of curing, wet-sand the repaired area with 3000-grit sandpaper and water, using light pressure to blend the new clear coat with the surrounding finish; keep the area lubricated and check frequently to avoid cutting through the new paint

13. Remove masking tape and plastic sheeting; wipe the area clean with a microfiber towel and inspect for uniformity

14. Attach a medium-grade foam pad to the DA polisher; apply a quarter-sized amount of polishing compound to the pad

15. Set the polisher to 3500 OPM; work the compound over the repaired area in overlapping passes, applying light pressure for 2–3 minutes until the surface gloss is restored

16. Switch to a finishing pad and repeat with a small amount of compound for final gloss enhancement; wipe off residue with a clean microfiber towel

17. Inspect the repair under natural and UV light for color match, gloss, and blend; repeat polishing if necessary for a seamless finish

18. Log the repair date, paint code, and products used in your maintenance record

Illustrations and diagrams

Cross-section diagram of paint layers (primer, base coat, clear coat) showing scratch penetration
Step-by-step illustration of masking, sanding, touch-up application, and clear coat blending
Diagram of DA polisher pad movement and pressure zones
UV flashlight inspection of clear coat blending

Practical expert tips

Always confirm your vehicle's paint code from the service manual or door jamb sticker to ensure an exact color match
Use a toothpick for ultra-fine scratches to avoid over-applying paint and creating raised spots
Allow touch-up paint and clear coat to cure for at least 24 hours before sanding or polishing for best results
Work in small sections to maintain control and prevent accidental damage to surrounding paint
Store touch-up paint and clear coat in a cool, dry place and tightly sealed to prevent thickening or contamination

Troubleshooting techniques

If the touch-up paint appears too thick or lumpy, thin with a drop of isopropyl alcohol and mix thoroughly before application
For visible paint edges after drying, gently feather with 3000-grit sandpaper and reapply clear coat as needed
If the repaired area looks dull after polishing, repeat with a finishing pad and less compound, increasing pad speed slightly
For color mismatch, remove the touch-up with isopropyl alcohol before clear coat application and start over with the correct paint code
If sanding through the new paint occurs, reapply color and clear coat, allowing full drying between steps

Security and preventive maintenance

Inspect exterior paint for new

scratches monthly and address promptly to prevent rust and further damage
Apply a high-quality wax or paint sealant every 3 months to protect the clear coat and minimize future scratches
Avoid automatic car washes with abrasive brushes; hand wash with a microfiber mitt and pH-neutral soap
Store touch-up materials in your garage or glove box for quick repairs of chips and scratches
Log all paint repairs and maintenance in your vehicle's record, noting location, date, and products used

4 INTERIOR AND EXTERIOR CARE

Carpet and Floor Mat Deep Clean with Odor Neutralization

Materials and Tools

- Heavy-duty wet/dry vacuum (12-gallon capacity, 5+ HP, with crevice and upholstery attachments)
- pH-balanced carpet and upholstery cleaner (enzyme-based, 32 oz spray bottle)
- Odor neutralizer spray (non-scented, non-masking, 16 oz, containing cyclodextrin or activated charcoal)
- Stiff-bristle carpet brush (synthetic, 8-inch handle, 2-inch bristle length)
- Soft-bristle detailing brush (synthetic, 1-inch diameter, for seams and edges)
- Microfiber towels (16x16 inch, 350+ GSM, 6 pieces)
- Hot water extractor or portable carpet cleaner (1-gallon tank, 1000W+ heating element)
- Rubber gloves (nitrile, 7 mil thickness)
- Plastic scraper (6-inch, for removing stuck debris)
- Spray bottle (32 oz, for water rinsing)
- Baking soda (sodium bicarbonate, 1 lb box)
- Large tarp or plastic sheeting (6x8 ft, for drying mats)
- Service manual (for mat removal instructions)

Step-by-step instructions

1. Park the vehicle on a level surface in a shaded, well-ventilated area with all doors open to maximize airflow and drying
2. Remove all floor mats, including front, rear, and cargo area mats; refer to the service manual for any clips or fasteners
3. Shake mats vigorously outdoors to dislodge loose dirt; use a plastic scraper to remove stuck-on debris or gum
4. Vacuum the mats and carpeted floor thoroughly using the wet/dry vacuum with crevice and upholstery attachments; pay special attention to seat rails, pedal areas, and under seats

5. Sprinkle a generous layer (1/4 cup per mat, 1/2 cup for cabin carpet) of baking soda over all carpeted surfaces; let sit for 30 minutes to absorb odors and moisture
6. Vacuum up all baking soda residue, ensuring no powder remains in seams or under seat tracks
7. Spray pH-balanced carpet and upholstery cleaner liberally onto mats and carpet (approx. 2–3 sprays per square foot); allow to dwell for 5 minutes to break down stains and organic matter
8. Agitate the cleaner into the fibers using a stiff-bristle carpet brush for mats and a soft-bristle detailing brush for seams, edges, and around seat mounts; use overlapping strokes and moderate pressure
9. For heavily soiled areas, repeat application and agitation until stains begin to lift
10. Fill the hot water extractor or portable carpet cleaner with hot tap water (120–140°F) and operate according to manufacturer instructions; extract the mats first, then the cabin carpet, making slow, overlapping passes to maximize dirt and moisture removal
11. For areas without an extractor, use a spray bottle filled with hot water to rinse, then blot with microfiber towels until no cleaner residue remains
12. Inspect all surfaces for remaining stains; spot-treat with additional cleaner and repeat extraction or blotting as needed
13. Spray odor neutralizer evenly over all cleaned carpet and mats (1–2 sprays per square foot); allow to air dry for 30–60 minutes
14. Place mats on a large tarp or plastic sheeting in a sunny, breezy area to dry completely; flip after 1 hour to ensure both sides dry
15. Leave vehicle doors open or use a portable fan to accelerate cabin carpet drying; avoid replacing mats until all surfaces are fully dry to prevent mildew
16. Reinstall mats according to the service manual, ensuring all clips and fasteners are secure
17. Log the cleaning date, products used, and any persistent stains or odors in your maintenance record

Illustrations and diagrams

Diagram of vehicle floor cross-section showing carpet, padding, and mat placement
Step-by-step illustration of mat removal, vacuuming, and extraction process
Diagram of baking soda application and vacuuming technique
Illustration of hot water extractor nozzle movement and overlap pattern

Practical expert tips

Always test carpet and upholstery cleaner on a hidden area to check for colorfastness before full application
Use separate brushes for mats and cabin carpet to avoid cross-contamination of dirt and debris
For pet hair, use a dampened rubber squeegee or pumice stone before vacuuming to lift embedded fur
If using a hot water extractor, empty and refill the tank with clean water after every two mats to prevent redepositing dirt
Store baking soda and odor neutralizer in your garage for quick

spot treatments between deep cleans

Troubleshooting techniques

If stains persist after extraction, apply a 1:1 mixture of cleaner and hot water, agitate, and extract again; repeat up to three times for stubborn spots
For lingering odors, sprinkle baking soda again after cleaning, let sit overnight, and vacuum thoroughly the next day
If carpet feels stiff after drying, mist lightly with clean water and brush with a soft-bristle brush to restore softness
If mats curl after drying, place them under a heavy, flat object for 24 hours to regain shape

Security and preventive maintenance

Deep clean carpets and mats every 6 months or after major spills to prevent mold and odor buildup
Use all-weather rubber mats during winter or rainy seasons to protect carpet from moisture and salt
Inspect for early signs of mildew (musty smell, discoloration) and address immediately with enzyme cleaner and thorough drying
Vacuum interior weekly to minimize dirt accumulation and extend the interval between deep cleans
Keep a small bottle of odor neutralizer and microfiber towel in your glove box for emergency spill response

Dashboard and Console Crack Repair with UV Protection

Materials and Tools

- Flexible dashboard repair kit (vinyl/leather compatible, includes filler compound, 1 oz, and grain texture sheets)
- UV-resistant dashboard topcoat (matte finish, 2 oz bottle, 99% UV block)
- Plastic spreader (3-inch width, flexible edge)
- 220-grit and 400-grit sandpaper (2 sheets each, 9x3.6 inch)
- Isopropyl alcohol (70%, 8 oz bottle)
- Microfiber towels (16x16 inch, 350+ GSM, lint-free, 2 pieces)
- Masking tape (1-inch wide, automotive grade)
- Heat gun (1200W, variable temperature, with concentrator nozzle)
- Fine-tip paintbrush (synthetic, 1/4 inch width)
- Utility knife (retractable, with fresh blade)
- Nitrile gloves (7 mil thickness)
- Service manual (for dashboard removal, if needed)
- UV flashlight (365 nm, for inspection)
- Small vacuum (handheld, 2+ HP, with crevice tool)

Step-by-step instructions

1. Park the vehicle in a shaded, well-ventilated area with ambient temperature between 65–80°F; avoid direct sunlight to prevent premature curing of repair compounds
2. Disconnect the negative battery terminal using a 10mm wrench to prevent accidental airbag deployment or electrical shorts
3. Clean the dashboard and console area thoroughly with isopropyl alcohol and a microfiber towel, removing all dust, oils, and protectant residues; allow to air dry for 5 minutes
4. Use masking tape to isolate a 2-inch perimeter around the crack or damaged area, protecting adjacent surfaces from filler and topcoat
5. Inspect the crack: for deep or wide cracks (over 1/16 inch), use a utility knife to slightly widen and undercut the edges, creating a V-groove for better filler adhesion; vacuum out debris with a crevice tool
6. Lightly sand the crack and surrounding area with 220-grit sandpaper to roughen the surface and improve filler bonding; wipe away dust with a clean microfiber towel
7. Wearing nitrile gloves, mix the flexible filler compound according to kit instructions; use the plastic spreader to press filler firmly into the crack, slightly overfilling to allow for shrinkage
8. Place a matching grain texture sheet over the filled area; use the heat gun set to 250°F, holding it 2–3 inches above the sheet, and move in slow, circular motions for 30–45 seconds to cure the filler and imprint the texture
9. Allow the area to cool for 5 minutes, then gently peel off the texture sheet; inspect for uniformity and repeat filler application and texturing if the crack is still visible or the surface is uneven
10. Sand the repaired area lightly with 400-grit sandpaper to blend edges with the surrounding dashboard; wipe clean with isopropyl alcohol
11. Using a fine-tip paintbrush, apply a thin, even layer of UV-resistant dashboard topcoat over the repaired area, feathering out 1 inch beyond the repair for seamless blending; allow to dry for 30 minutes
12. Apply a second coat of UV topcoat if needed for full coverage and maximum protection; allow to cure for 1 hour before removing masking tape
13. Inspect the repair under a UV flashlight to confirm even coverage and absence of exposed filler; touch up with additional topcoat if necessary
14. Reconnect the negative battery terminal and test all dashboard functions to ensure proper operation
15. Log the repair date, products used, and location of the repair in your maintenance record

Illustrations and diagrams

Cross-section diagram of dashboard crack showing V-groove preparation and filler application
Step-by-step illustration of masking, filler spreading, texture sheet placement, and heat gun curing
Diagram of UV topcoat application and feathering technique
UV flashlight inspection of repaired area for coverage

Practical expert tips

Always match the grain texture sheet to your dashboard's original pattern for a nearly invisible repair; test on a hidden area if unsure

Use a heat gun with a concentrator nozzle for precise, even heating—avoid overheating, which can warp plastic or vinyl

For color-matched repairs, mix dashboard dye into the filler compound before application, following kit instructions

Store unused filler and topcoat in a cool, dry place with lids tightly sealed to prevent hardening

Keep a UV-resistant dashboard cover or sunshade in your vehicle to further protect against future cracking

Troubleshooting techniques

If the filler shrinks below the surface after curing, reapply a thin layer and repeat the texturing and curing process

For visible repair edges, feather with 400-grit sandpaper and reapply topcoat, blending outward for a seamless finish

If the texture imprint is uneven, reheat gently with the heat gun and press the texture sheet again while the filler is still warm

For color mismatch, apply a dashboard dye or paint over the cured topcoat, matching the original color as closely as possible

If the repaired area feels sticky after curing, allow additional drying time or use a fan to accelerate solvent evaporation

Security and preventive maintenance

Inspect the dashboard and console for new cracks or UV damage every 3 months, especially in summer or high-sun regions

Apply a UV-resistant protectant (water-based, non-greasy) to the entire dashboard every 2 months to maintain flexibility and color

Use windshield sunshades whenever parked outdoors to reduce interior temperatures and UV exposure

Avoid placing heavy or sharp objects on the dashboard to prevent new cracks or dents

Log all repairs and maintenance in your vehicle's record, noting the location, date, and products used for future reference

Convertible Top Cleaning, Waterproofing and Zipper Service

Materials and Tools

- pH-neutral convertible top cleaner (fabric or vinyl-specific, 16 oz spray bottle)
- Soft-bristle convertible top brush (synthetic, 10-inch handle, flagged bristles)
- Microfiber towels (16x16 inch, 350+ GSM, 4 pieces)

- Low-pressure garden hose with adjustable spray nozzle (max 40 psi)
- Convertible top protectant/waterproofer (aerosol or pump, 16 oz, UV-resistant, fabric or vinyl-specific)
- Painter's tape (1-inch wide, automotive grade, for masking bodywork and glass)
- Zipper lubricant (PTFE or silicone-based, 0.5 oz tube or stick)
- Soft toothbrush (nylon bristles)
- Compressed air canister (10 oz, with straw nozzle)
- Nitrile gloves (7 mil thickness)
- Service manual (for top operation and care recommendations)

Step-by-step instructions

1. Park the vehicle in a shaded, dust-free area with ambient temperature between 60–80°F; ensure the top is fully closed and latched
2. Rinse the convertible top thoroughly with a low-pressure garden hose, using a wide spray pattern to avoid forcing water through seams or seals
3. Apply painter's tape along all edges where the top meets painted body panels, glass, and trim to prevent cleaner or protectant overspray
4. Spray pH-neutral convertible top cleaner evenly over the entire surface (approx. 2-3 sprays per square foot); allow to dwell for 3-5 minutes to loosen dirt and contaminants
5. Gently scrub the top using a soft-bristle convertible top brush, working in straight lines parallel to the fabric grain or vinyl texture; use light to moderate pressure to avoid damaging fibers or stitching
6. For seams and stubborn stains, use a soft toothbrush with additional cleaner, agitating gently in small circular motions
7. Rinse the top thoroughly with the garden hose, ensuring all cleaner residue is removed; avoid directing water at seals or zippers
8. Blot excess water with clean microfiber towels, pressing rather than rubbing to prevent surface abrasion; allow the top to air dry completely (30–60 minutes)
9. Once dry, mask off all surrounding bodywork, glass, and trim with painter's tape and towels to protect from protectant overspray
10. Shake the convertible top protectant/waterproofer well; hold the nozzle 8–12 inches from the surface and apply in overlapping, even passes (approx. 1 oz per 5 sq ft); avoid saturating seams
11. Allow the first coat to dry for 10–15 minutes, then apply a second coat for maximum water repellency and UV protection
12. Remove all masking tape and towels after the final coat is dry to the touch (usually 30 minutes)
13. Inspect all zippers for dirt, debris, or resistance; use a compressed air canister to blow out dust and grit from zipper teeth
14. Apply a thin bead of PTFE or silicone-based zipper lubricant along the entire length of each zipper; work the zipper back and forth several times to distribute lubricant evenly
15. Wipe away any excess lubricant with a microfiber towel to prevent transfer to the top or interior
16. Log the cleaning, waterproofing, and zipper service date, products used, and any observed wear in your maintenance record

Illustrations and diagrams

Diagram of convertible top cross-section showing fabric/vinyl layers, seams, and zipper locations
Step-by-step illustration of masking, cleaning, and protectant application technique
Close-up diagram of zipper lubrication and debris removal with compressed air and toothbrush

Practical expert tips

Always use a cleaner and protectant specifically formulated for your top material (fabric or vinyl); check the owner's manual or service manual for compatibility
Clean and waterproof the top at least twice a year, or after exposure to tree sap, bird droppings, or heavy rain
For stubborn stains (mildew, sap), spot-treat with a 1:1 mixture of cleaner and warm water, agitate gently, and rinse thoroughly
Avoid automatic car washes with spinning brushes, which can damage convertible tops and zippers
Store zipper lubricant in your glove box for quick touch-ups if zippers become stiff or noisy

Troubleshooting techniques

If water beads do not form after protectant application, repeat with a second or third coat, allowing full drying between coats
For persistent zipper resistance, clean thoroughly with a toothbrush and reapply lubricant; if still stiff, inspect for bent or damaged teeth and consult a professional
If the top develops leaks at seams, inspect for worn stitching or failed seam sealer; apply a seam sealer compatible with your top material as a temporary fix
For white residue or streaks after protectant application, buff gently with a dry microfiber towel and reduce product amount on future applications

Security and preventive maintenance

Inspect the convertible top monthly for signs of wear, fading, or seam separation; address issues promptly to prevent leaks and costly repairs
Keep the top clean and free of debris to prevent mold, mildew, and premature fabric or vinyl degradation
Lubricate all zippers every 3 months or after exposure to rain, dust, or road salt to ensure smooth operation and prevent binding
Avoid folding or stowing the top when wet to prevent mildew and odor buildup
Log all maintenance activities, including cleaning, waterproofing, and zipper service, in your vehicle's record for warranty and resale purposes

Exterior Trim and Chrome Polish with Pitting Repair

THE CAR MAINTENANCE AND REPAIR BIBLE

Materials and Tools

- Non-abrasive chrome and metal polish (liquid or paste, 8 oz bottle, ammonia-free)
- Fine-grade #0000 steel wool (ultra-fine, oil-free, 16-pad pack)
- Microfiber towels (16x16 inch, 350+ GSM, lint-free, 4 pieces)
- Plastic trim restorer (silicone-based, UV-resistant, 8 oz bottle)
- Soft foam applicator pads (3-inch diameter, closed-cell, 2 pieces)
- Detailing brush (synthetic bristles, 1-inch width, 6-inch handle)
- Isopropyl alcohol (70%, 8 oz bottle)
- Masking tape (1-inch wide, automotive grade)
- Nitrile gloves (7 mil thickness)
- Toothpicks (wooden, pointed tip, 20 pieces)
- Cotton swabs (6-inch, wooden stick, 20 pieces)
- Small plastic container (8 oz, for soaking)
- Chrome touch-up pen (color-matched, 0.5 oz, for deep pits)
- UV flashlight (365 nm, for inspection)
- Service manual (for trim removal, if needed)

Step-by-step instructions

1. Park the vehicle in a shaded, dust-free area with ambient temperature between 60–80°F; ensure all trim and chrome surfaces are cool to the touch
2. Wash the exterior trim and chrome thoroughly with car shampoo and water, rinse, and dry with a clean microfiber towel to remove all dirt and road film
3. Use masking tape to protect adjacent paint, rubber, and plastic surfaces from accidental polish or steel wool contact; apply a 1-inch border around all chrome and trim pieces
4. Inspect chrome for pitting, rust spots, and oxidation using a UV flashlight; mark areas with visible pitting for targeted repair
5. For light pitting and surface rust, don nitrile gloves and gently rub the affected area with #0000 steel wool, using light, straight-line strokes; avoid circular motions to prevent swirl marks
6. Wipe away loosened rust and debris with a dry microfiber towel; repeat steel wool application as needed until pits are minimized and surface feels smooth
7. For deeper pits, use a toothpick to carefully remove any loose rust or debris from the pit; soak a cotton swab in isopropyl alcohol and clean inside each pit to remove contaminants
8. If bare metal is exposed in deep pits, apply a chrome touch-up pen following manufacturer instructions; allow to dry for 30 minutes before proceeding
9. Apply a small amount (pea-sized) of non-abrasive chrome polish to a foam applicator pad; work the polish into the chrome using overlapping,

straight-line motions, focusing on pitted and dull areas

10. Allow the polish to haze (per product instructions, typically 2–5 minutes), then buff off with a clean microfiber towel, turning frequently to avoid smearing residue
11. For intricate trim or tight corners, use a detailing brush or cotton swab with a drop of polish to reach all crevices; wipe clean with a microfiber towel
12. Inspect the chrome under a UV flashlight to confirm all pitting and oxidation have been addressed; repeat polish application if necessary for maximum shine
13. For exterior plastic trim adjacent to chrome, apply a thin bead of plastic trim restorer to a clean foam applicator pad; spread evenly along the trim, working in 12-inch sections
14. Allow the trim restorer to penetrate for 5 minutes, then buff off excess with a separate microfiber towel to prevent streaking or residue
15. Remove all masking tape and inspect for polish or restorer residue on paint or glass; clean any spots with isopropyl alcohol and a microfiber towel
16. Log the date, products used, and any persistent pitting or damage in your maintenance record

Illustrations and diagrams

Cross-section diagram of chrome trim showing pitting, rust removal, and touch-up process
Step-by-step illustration of masking, steel wool application, and polish technique
Diagram of plastic trim restorer application and buffing method

Practical expert tips

Always use #0000 ultra-fine steel wool for chrome; coarser grades will scratch and dull the finish
Test chrome polish on a hidden area first to ensure compatibility and avoid discoloration
For stubborn pitting, alternate between steel wool and polish, working in small sections to avoid over-polishing
Store chrome polish and trim restorer in a cool, dry place with caps tightly sealed to prevent drying out
Use a UV flashlight to spot early signs of pitting or oxidation before they become visible in daylight

Troubleshooting techniques

If pitting remains after steel wool and polish, use a chrome touch-up pen to fill and seal the pits, preventing further rust
For streaky or hazy chrome after polishing, reapply a small amount of polish and buff with a clean, dry microfiber towel
If plastic trim appears blotchy after restorer application, wipe with a damp microfiber towel and reapply a thin, even coat
For polish residue on paint or glass, remove immediately with isopropyl alcohol and a clean towel to prevent staining

Security and preventive maintenance

Inspect all chrome and exterior trim monthly for new pitting, rust, or fading; address issues promptly to prevent permanent damage
Apply a non-abrasive chrome polish and plastic trim restorer every 3 months, or after exposure to road

salt, rain, or harsh chemicals

Use a car cover or park in a garage to minimize environmental exposure and slow the development of pitting and oxidation

Avoid using abrasive cleaners, harsh chemicals, or automatic car washes with stiff brushes on chrome and trim surfaces

Log all maintenance activities, including polish and restorer applications, in your vehicle's record for warranty and resale purposes

Chapter 14: Troubleshooting, Resources, Next Steps

If you handle your own car maintenance, you can save money and gain confidence, but you should start with a clear plan. Begin troubleshooting by defining the symptom precisely. Write down when it happens, the conditions, and any unusual noises, smells, or warning lights. For example, if the car makes a strange noise, note whether it occurs during acceleration, braking, or idling, and record how often and how loud it is. Once you understand the problem, use a generic **OBD-II reader** to scan for trouble codes. That tool captures freeze-frame data—engine temperature, RPM, and vehicle speed at the time of the fault—which helps narrow the cause.

Before you perform complex diagnostics, verify the basics. Confirm battery voltage is above **12.4 volts**, keep grounds clean and tight, and test fuses and relays for continuity with a multimeter. Inspect fluid levels and condition—look for contamination such as discoloration or particles—and watch for leaks. Vacuum leaks often cause rough idle or misfires, so inspect hoses and connections around the intake manifold and throttle body. If the issue persists, reproduce it with short, controlled tests to avoid further damage and note any changes in performance or symptoms.

Isolate the affected system—fuel, air, ignition, cooling, brakes, charging, starting, or suspension—and focus on the most likely, cost-effective fixes first. For a misfire or rough idle, look for vacuum leaks, assess ignition coils and spark plugs, and use a scanner to read fuel trims to determine if the engine runs rich or lean. If the car won't start, determine whether it cranks, then perform a spark test and measure fuel pressure to distinguish ignition from fuel delivery problems. For overheating, inspect coolant level, fan operation, and thermostat or radiator flow to confirm the cooling system works properly.

Recognize when to stop and get professional help. Safety systems such as airbags, high-voltage components in hybrids or EVs, fuel leaks, structural rust, and complex engine or transmission problems should be handled by experts. Attempting these repairs without proper tools and training can cause more damage, create safety hazards, and lead to expensive repairs or injury.

Build your skills and toolset by acquiring essential diagnostic equipment: a quality **OBD-II scanner with live data**, a multimeter for electrical work, a torque wrench for accurate fastener tightening, and pressure or vacuum gauges for fluid system checks. A service jack and stands are essential for safe undercarriage work and proper inspections. On every job, learn one new diagnostic feature—*fuel trims*, misfire counters, or similar—to broaden your troubleshooting ability.

Use OEM service portals, repair databases like ALLDATA or Mitchell DIY, and parts-brand technical sheets for detailed procedures and specifications. Access Technical Service Bulletins and recalls via NHTSA or manufacturer sites for important updates. ASE A1–A8 guides cover core automotive fundamentals from engine performance to electrical systems. Reputable online channels and forums can help when they provide verified procedures and torque specs; avoid guidance that lacks data or specifications, which can cause costly errors.

Choose OE or reputable aftermarket parts that meet or exceed OEM standards so they match DOT ratings, fluid viscosity, and other requirements for your vehicle. Compare old and new parts before installation to confirm compatibility, and keep a maintenance log with receipts and torque values for future reference. That log helps track repairs and service intervals.

Create a practical 30/60/90-day plan:

- In the first 30 days, assemble a basic toolkit, scanner, and safety gear like gloves and goggles. Start a maintenance log and run baseline checks on fluids, belts, hoses, brakes, tires, and the battery, fixing minor issues early.
- By 60 days, handle intermediate tasks: replace spark plugs and filters, service brakes, and change coolant—follow torque and bleed specs to ensure proper function.
- At 90 days, perform electrical testing, vacuum or boost leak detection, and smoke testing to find hidden problems. Subscribe to service information specific to your car and set up a seasonal preventive checklist covering oil and brake fluid intervals, tire rotation and alignment checks, and inspections of cabin filters, wipers, and lighting.

Adopt ongoing habits to keep your vehicle performing reliably. Scan and record codes before disconnecting the battery to preserve diagnostic data, tighten fasteners to specified torque to prevent failures, recheck fluid levels after drives to catch leaks early, and re-torque wheels after 50–100 kilometers for safety. Schedule periodic tool calibration to keep measurements accurate.

www.ingramcontent.com/pod-product-compliance
Lightning Source LLC
Chambersburg PA
CBHW051409070526
44584CB00023B/3351